MW01616574

THE LANDSCAPE PHOTOGRAPHER'S GUIDE

PHOTOGRAPHING
Rocky Mountain National Park

ERIK STENSLAND

Morning Light Photography
P.O. Box 2843
Estes Park, CO 80517
www.ImagesofRMNP.com & www.MorningLight.us

Book design by Jerry Dorris, AuthorSupport.com
Edited by Janna Nysewander

ISBN: 978-0-9969626-4-3
Printed in South Korea

Front cover: June in Moraine Park.
Back cover: Aspen trees near Lily Lake

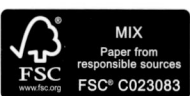

MIX
Paper from
responsible sources
FSC® C023083
www.fsc.org

Printed using soy-based inks—Sustainable Manufacturing—Renewable Resources

May you find beauty everywhere
and hear its quiet message.

CONTENTS

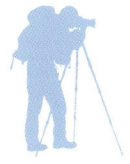

INTRODUCTION

Are you planning a trip to Rocky Mountain National Park and wanting to know where to photograph? Then this is the guide for you. It includes many of the most accessible photo locations in the park, together with advice on when, where, and how to capture these photogenic places.

Since 2004, Rocky Mountain National Park has been my main area of focus. During these years, I have explored and photographed nearly every corner of the park and become attuned to its cycles and moods. In these pages, I'll be sharing with you much of what I have learned.

The locations in this book are listed by their proximity to primary park roads. Grab a map at the entrance station to go along with this guide or download one of the many maps available online and you'll be ready to go.

With nearly 150 alpine lakes, over 400 miles of rivers and streams, and 60 peaks over 12,000 feet, there is more to photograph in RMNP than I could fit into one short book. My encouragement to you is to take what I've written and use it as a starting point. Look around you and you'll find many additional vantage points and opportunities. Allow your own creativity to guide you.

For further ideas and inspiration, visit my gallery in downtown Estes Park or my website www. ImagesofRMNP.com, which features over a thousand photographs of this amazing park. The website is divided into seasons and locations, allowing you to get a better idea of what a certain place looks like or which things are good to photograph during each season.

I hope you have a very successful visit to RMNP!

Erik Stensland

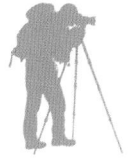

THE BASICS

Before we begin talking about photo locations, let's start by reviewing some of the basics of landscape photography. If you are an advanced photographer you may want to skip some parts of this chapter, but please take a moment to at least review the safety, environmental, and etiquette sections.

SAFETY

When doing landscape photography, safety must be a high priority. Hiking in the wilderness comes with risks, particularly if you are out before sunrise and after sunset. Proper preparation will greatly reduce your risk of encountering problems and will help you stay safe. Here are some tips to help you prepare.

Since cell phones do not work in most areas of the park, make sure someone knows exactly where you are going and when they should expect you to return. Then stick to your plan as closely as you can. If at all possible, hike with a companion. Also, stay on established trails. Stay below tree line during storms—which typically arrive in midafternoon during the summer season—as lightning is a major killer.

Be aware that many of the trails start at an elevation of more than 9,000 feet. You need to be in good health and acclimatized to the elevation before attempting any longer hikes. Drinking plenty of water both before and after your arrival will help your body adjust to the elevation. If you experience dizziness, headache, nausea, difficulty breathing, or extreme fatigue, quickly head to a lower elevation, as this may be the onset of altitude sickness, which can become life-threatening if ignored.

Finally, keep these 10 essentials with you at all times:

- navigation (topographical map and compass)
- sun protection (sunglasses and sunscreen)
- insulation (extra layers)
- first-aid supplies
- fire (waterproof matches/lighter/candles)
- repair kit and tools

List continues on next page

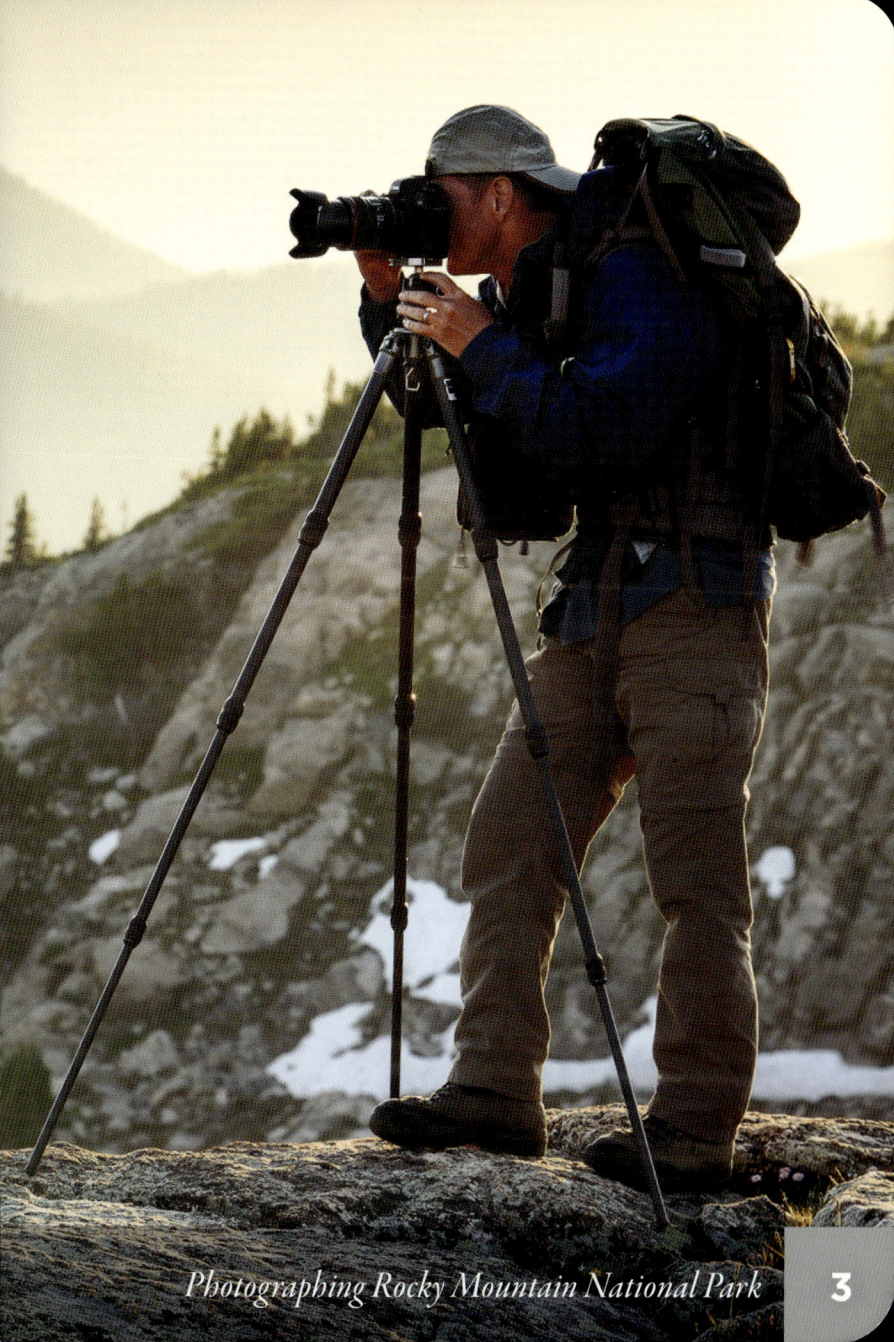

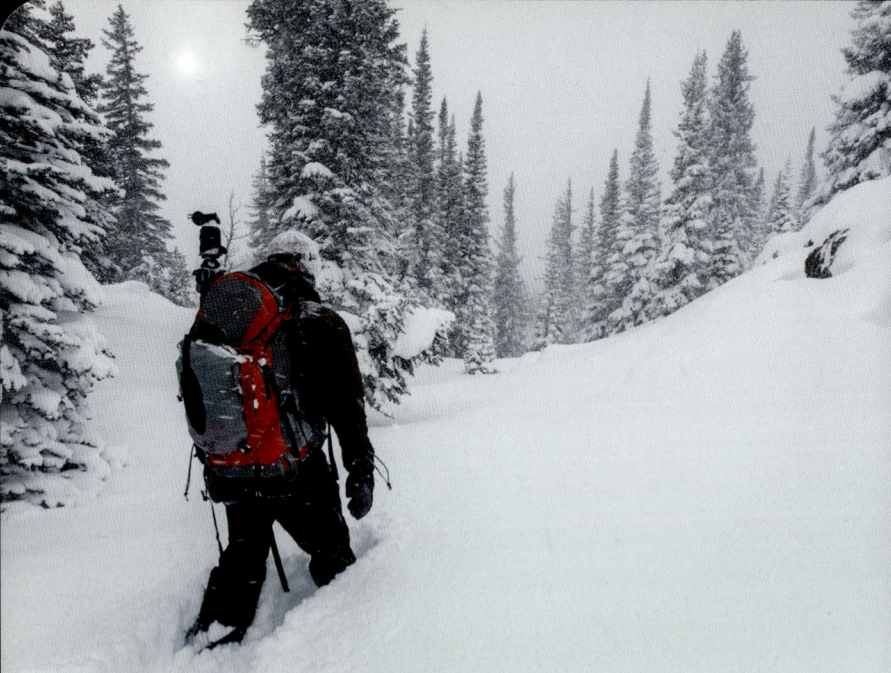

- nutrition (extra food)
- hydration (extra water)
- emergency shelter (space blanket)
- illumination (head lamp)

The last item is especially important, since landscape photography often involves being at locations before sunrise and after sunset. You must have a good head lamp with you, as well as extra batteries. I always carry two head lamps and additional batteries.

If you follow these very basic precautions, you will

have a safer and more successful wilderness experience.

GEAR

Most people think the key to creating amazing photos is having expensive equipment, but that's about as true as saying expensive cooking utensils make you a good cook. The key is in knowing how to use what you have.

Ideally, I recommend that you have a camera that allows you some manual control, such as a DSLR. If you are shooting with your phone, download an app that will allow you more control over the camera. If you are shopping for a camera, both Nikon and Canon make excellent entry-level DSLRs. These entry-level cameras will be more than adequate for most photographers.

The other tool you must have if you want to get the highest-quality images is a sturdy tripod. There really is no such thing as a good lightweight tripod. You want one that has a bit of weight so that it maintains good stability. Use it for all your photos, especially those taken at sunrise and sunset, to create crystal-clear images.

Another tool I recommend is a 3-stop soft graduated neutral density filter. This resin rectangle will help you balance the brightness of the sky with the darkness of

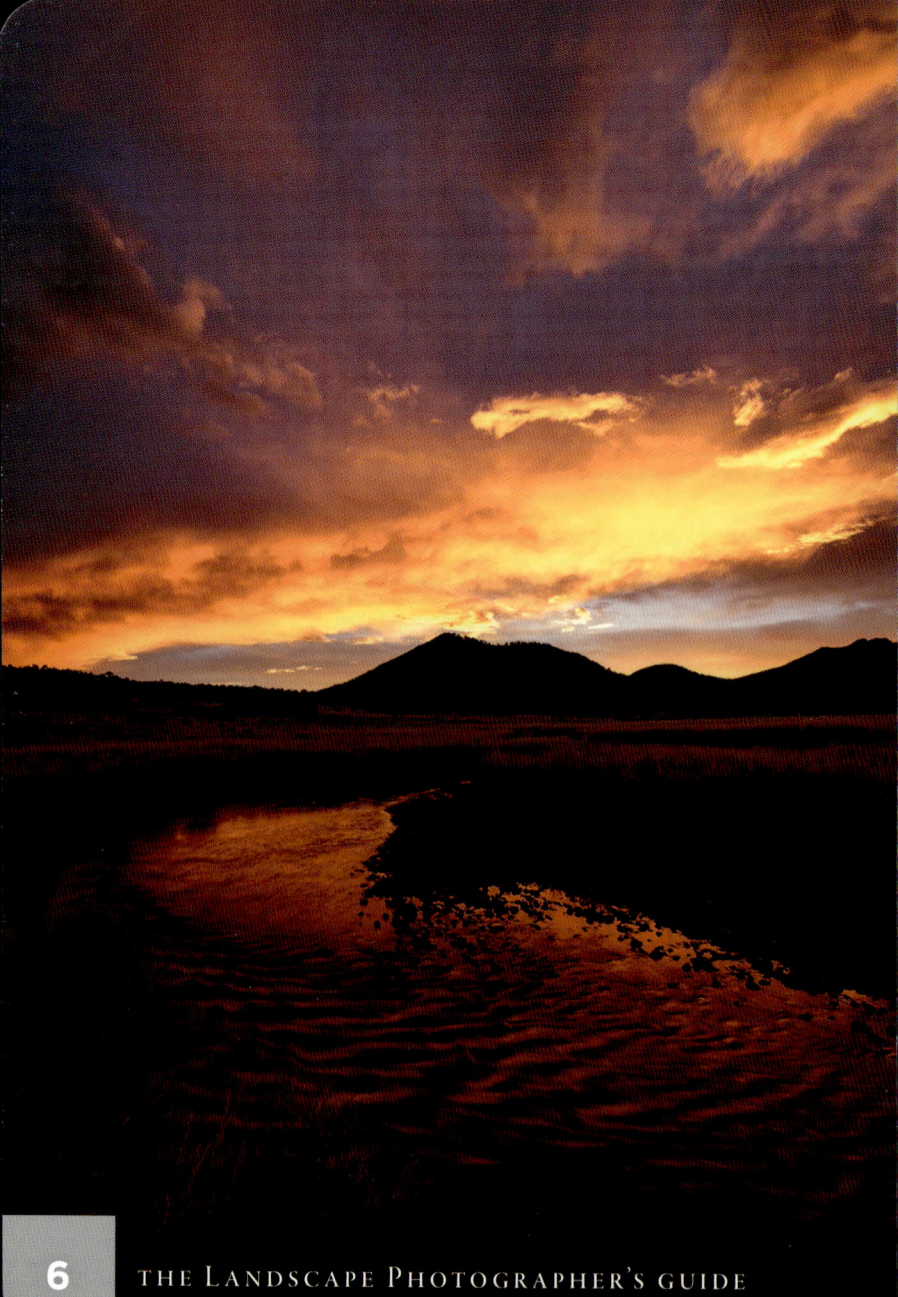

THE LANDSCAPE PHOTOGRAPHER'S GUIDE

the ground to help you create images that look more like what your eye can see. The best ones are made by Singh-Ray, but a more affordable option is provided by Hitech. Alternatively, you can learn to blend multiple exposures to get similar results. Adobe Photoshop Lightroom has a photo merge feature to help with this process.

LIGHTING

The "secret" to creating amazing photos is amazing light. *Photography* comes from the Greek language and means "drawing with light." Light is the most important component to any photograph. I often have people come into my gallery complaining that they stood in the same spot as I did, but their photos don't look at all like mine. The difference is usually in the light.

The warmest and most colorful light can be found at sunrise or sunset, depending on your location. Most of my photos are taken within fifteen minutes of these times in order to take advantage of this special light. Here in Rocky Mountain National Park, most places are best at sunrise due to the nature of the topography, but I do list a couple of sunset locations in this book as well.

The quality of the light depends on many factors. One

of the most important of these factors is the location of the clouds. If the sun is blocked as it sets or rises, you won't get the warm light. Smoke or haze can also affect the quality of the light. Watch the weather forecasts closely, as you want clouds over the mountains but none on the horizon.

I rely on two primary tools to help me find the best light. The first is a program called the Photographer's Ephemeris,* together with its inbuilt Skyfire program. These help me determine the direction of light on the peak and predict the likelihood of good light. The second is a website for cloud predictions called ClearDarkSky. Becoming a student of light is the most important key to becoming a good landscape photographer.

COMPOSITION

One of the biggest mistakes people make when taking a photo is trying to include everything in one shot. A great way to improve your photography is to choose just one subject for your photo, whether it is an individual elk, a particular mountain, or one wildflower. Zooming in so that your subject fills most of the frame will help create a much more interesting image. Try to simplify your image as much as possible. Look at the image and see if there is anything that distracts you from your subject. If there is, change your position to eliminate the distracting object.

You can make your composition more interesting by placing your subject somewhere other than in the very center of the frame. One approach that I sometimes use is to identify my subject, such as a mountain, and then find leading lines that will point toward it. They may be logs in the water, stones in a line, tree tops, or even clouds. Anything that will put the emphasis on your subject can be helpful.

As you look at your composition, take note if there are any areas that lack interest and then try to minimize those areas. Cloudless blue skies look beautiful to the eye, but when seen in a photo they just feel empty. Change your composition to minimize any empty spaces.

Finally, spend time looking at photos and identify ones that move you emotionally. Look at how they were composed and notice the quality and direction of the light. Such study will help you become a better photographer.

If you want to learn more about any of these areas, then you might enjoy my e-book: *Getting Started in Landscape Photography*, which can be found on my ImagesofRMNP.com website.

ENVIRONMENT

Over the last few years we've seen an increasing number of visitors to Rocky Mountain National Park. The environmental impact on the park has been significant. Trails are appearing where previously there were none, grass is being trampled down to dirt, and the signs of human impact can be felt throughout the park. You can help to reduce the impact of your visit by staying on the official trails. If you do step off of a trail, try to walk only on hard surfaces such as rocks or where nothing is growing. It doesn't take more than a few footsteps on vegetation to wear it down to dirt.

If you find a unique vantage point, instead of sharing the location with the world, keep it for yourself so that others don't follow you and trample that area. The locations in this book have all been selected so as to give you some great photo locations while at the same time protecting the park. In fact, I am often quite concerned about the impact my photos may have on this national treasure, so in discussion with national park rangers, we've come to the agreement that I will not publicize any location that is not photographed from an official trail. You might want to consider doing the same.

ETIQUETTE

Photographers have a tendency to get so focused on a photo they are trying to capture that they forget to pay attention to the rest of the world and what is happening around them. I've seen photographers get so lost in capturing a shot that they do things they would otherwise never consider doing such as stepping in areas that damage the environment, setting up right in front of other photographers, or backing up near the edge of a cliff. With a little forethought and care we can avoid developing tunnel vision.

When photographing in public places like our national parks, it is vital that we know how to shoot with other photographers. In some of the locations listed in this book, you will find other photographers trying to shoot the same scene as you. A little courtesy goes a long way and makes for a friendly rather than adversarial situation. Standard etiquette is that the first person to arrive at a scene should be given first choice of their shooting location. If you arrive after them, try to avoid getting in their shot and ask them to let you know if you step into their field of view. If you arrive first, be polite and at some point give other photographers a chance to shoot from your spot or within your field of view. A little give-and-take can help everyone to have a good experience.

Another important part of photographer etiquette involves where we stand to take a photo. The National Park Service strives to protect our national parks from being damaged by the large number of visitors. If you see a sign telling you to stay on the trail or to stay off of an area, please respect this. Your photo is not worth the damage to these areas. We as landscape photographers take photos to celebrate the beauty and do not want to be part of its destruction. In Rocky, it is especially important to be mindful in the tundra areas, where an errant footstep could destroy plants that may take hundreds of years to re-grow in this fragile environment. 🚶

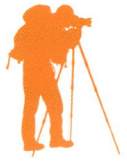

FALL RIVER ROAD

Elk-filled meadows, deep forests, cascades, waterfalls, and lofty tundra all lie along Fall River Road. Completed in 1920, it was the first road in Rocky Mountain National Park to reach above the trees. It takes visitors from Estes Park up to the Alpine Visitor Center at nearly 12,000 feet above sea level. Along the way, there is a lot of beauty to enjoy.

HORSESHOE PARK

Not far from Estes Park lies the northeast entrance to the national park on Fall River Road. About half a mile after entering the park, you reach a large meadow where elk can often be found grazing and enjoying the sunshine. This is Horseshoe Park, named for the many

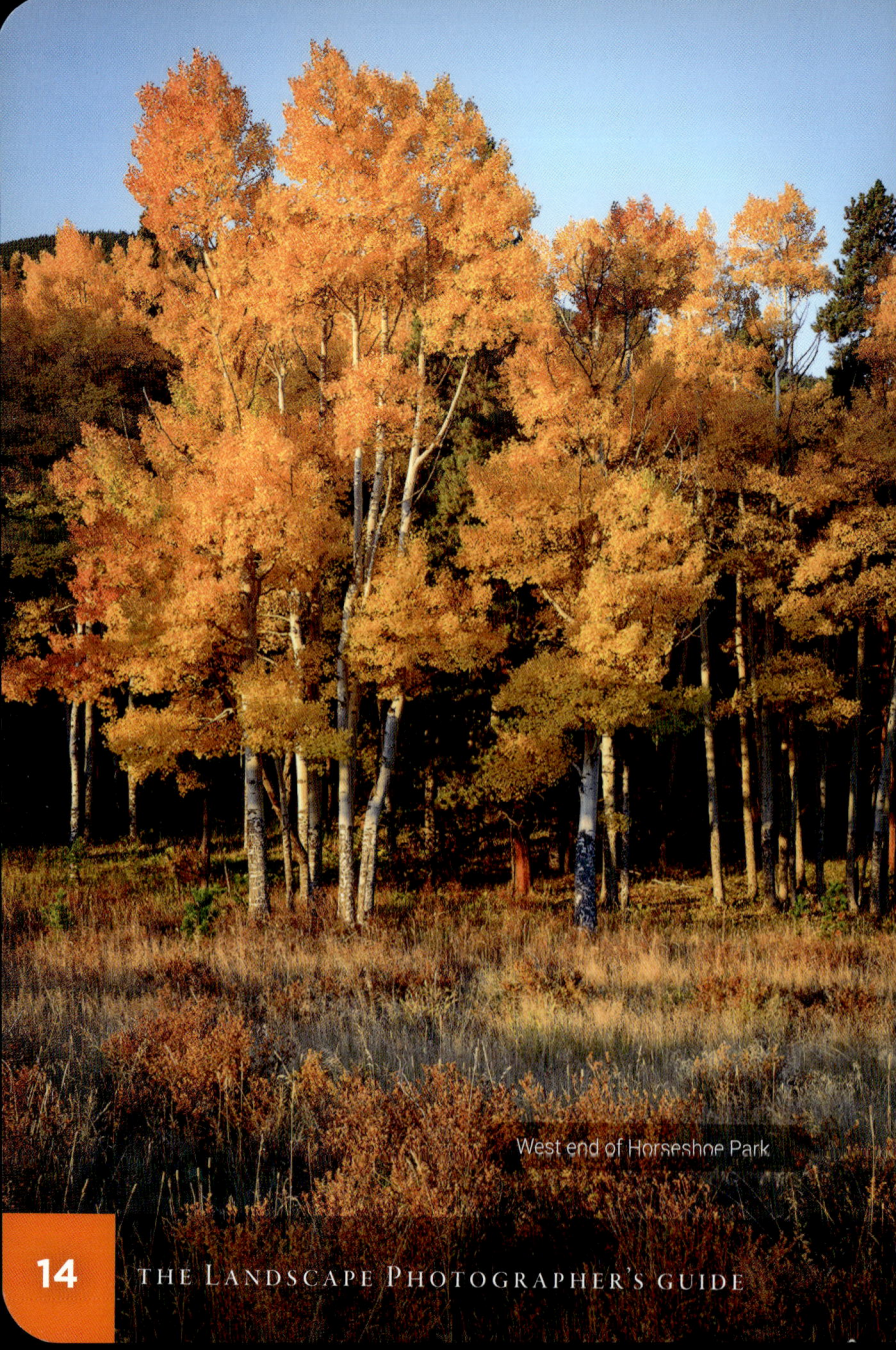

West end of Horseshoe Park

THE LANDSCAPE PHOTOGRAPHER'S GUIDE

U-shaped turns of Fall River as it makes its way through the meadow.

Large areas on the east end of this meadow have been fenced off, making them a bit less photogenic than they were previously. These enclosures were created to protect certain areas of vegetation such as aspen trees and willows from the large population of elk. Take a moment to notice the difference between what is growing inside of these enclosures and what is growing outside of them.

Your first stop in Horseshoe Park should be Sheep Lakes. There is a view from the west end of the parking lot where you can capture the little pond and some of the Mummy Range. If you're lucky, you may even see some bighorn sheep grazing here.

Follow the road to the west and it will soon take a sharp turn to the left. Shortly after this the road crosses a small bridge. From this bridge you can photograph Fall River winding its way up toward the Chapin, Chiquita, and Ypsilon peaks. This is especially beautiful in the spring and autumn but is worth photographing all year long.

Continue past the bridge heading south and you will find numerous possibilities on the west side of the road using the meadow, the aspen trees, and the peaks behind them to create nice compositions. This area can

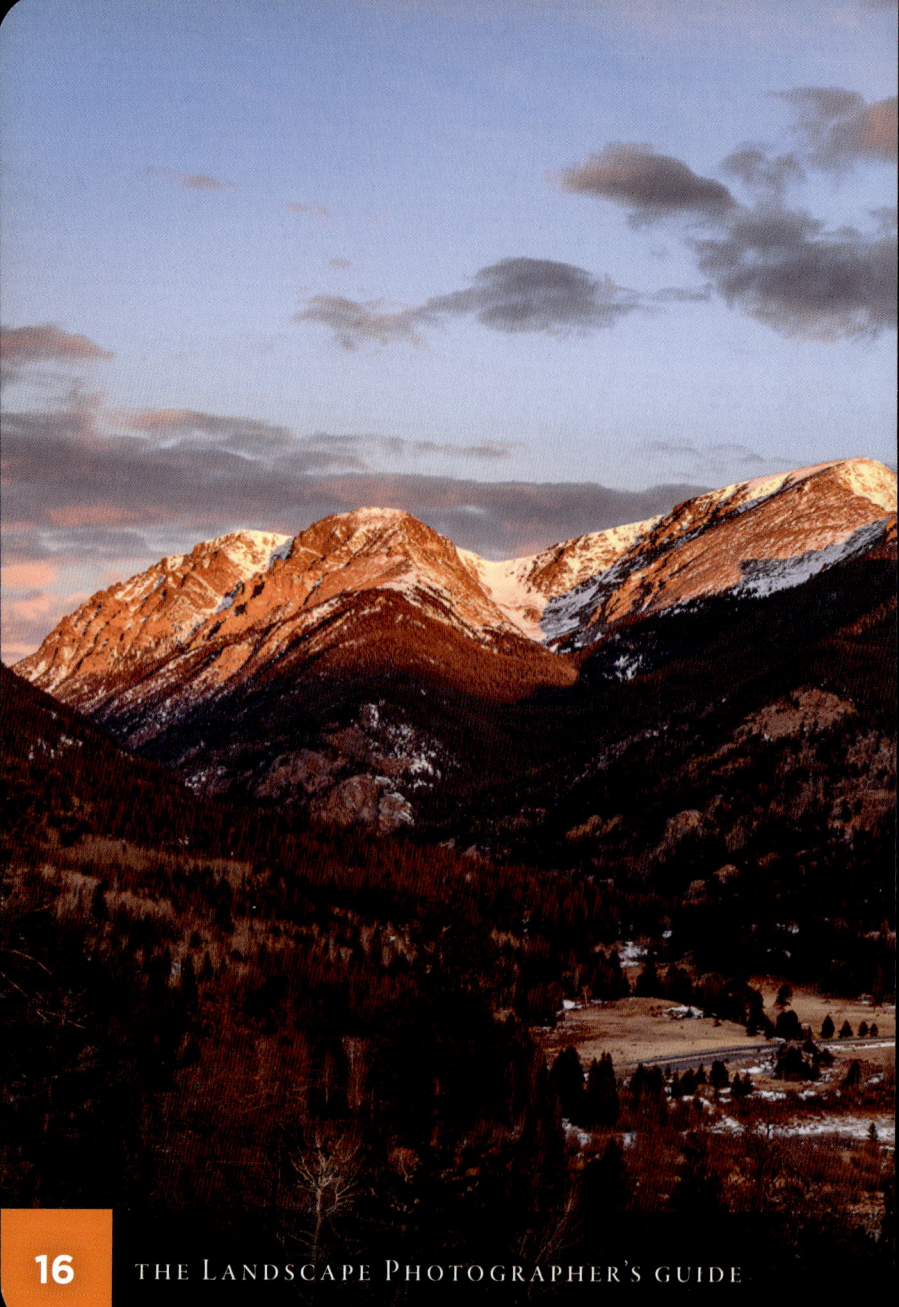

THE LANDSCAPE PHOTOGRAPHER'S GUIDE

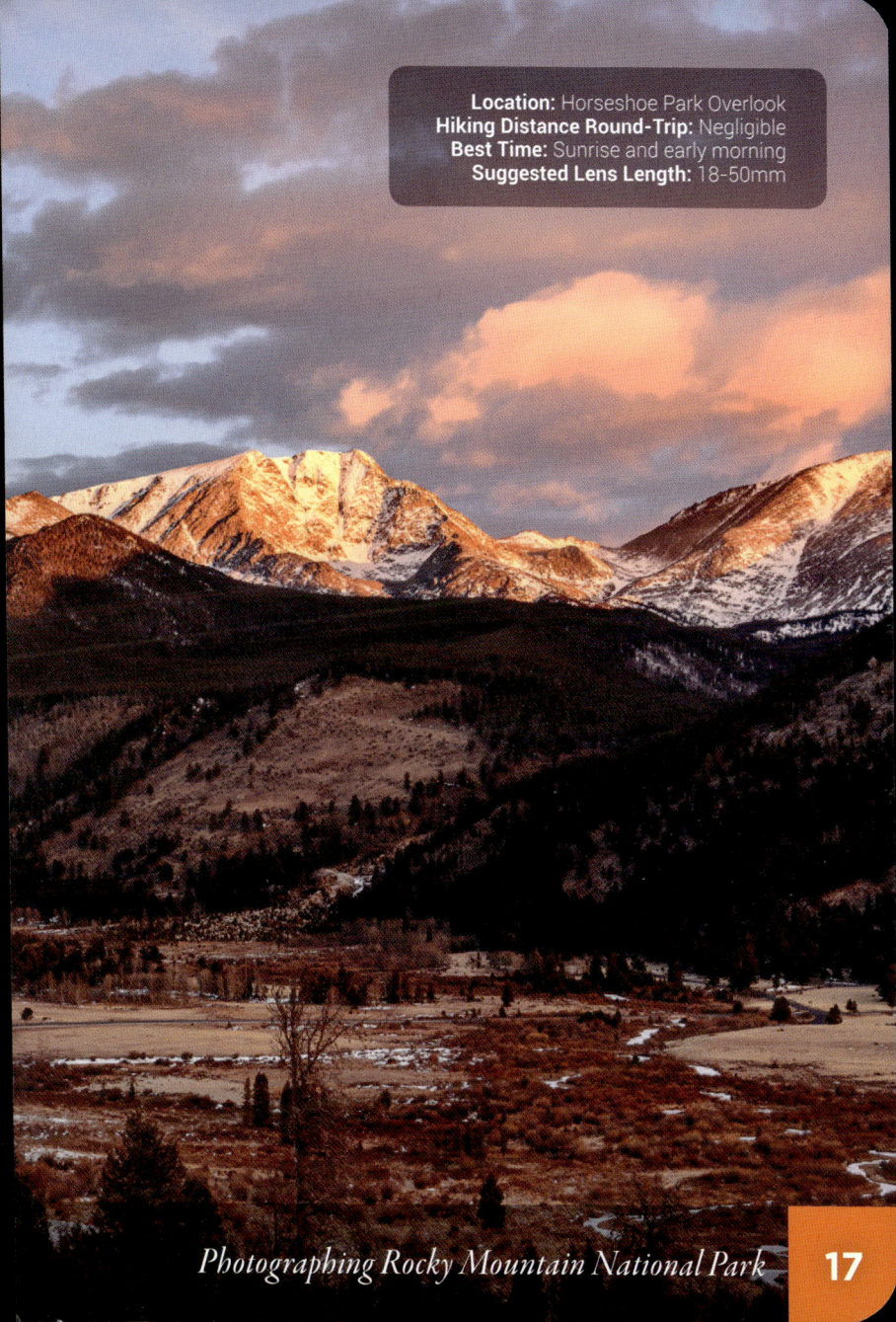

Location: Horseshoe Park Overlook
Hiking Distance Round-Trip: Negligible
Best Time: Sunrise and early morning
Suggested Lens Length: 18-50mm

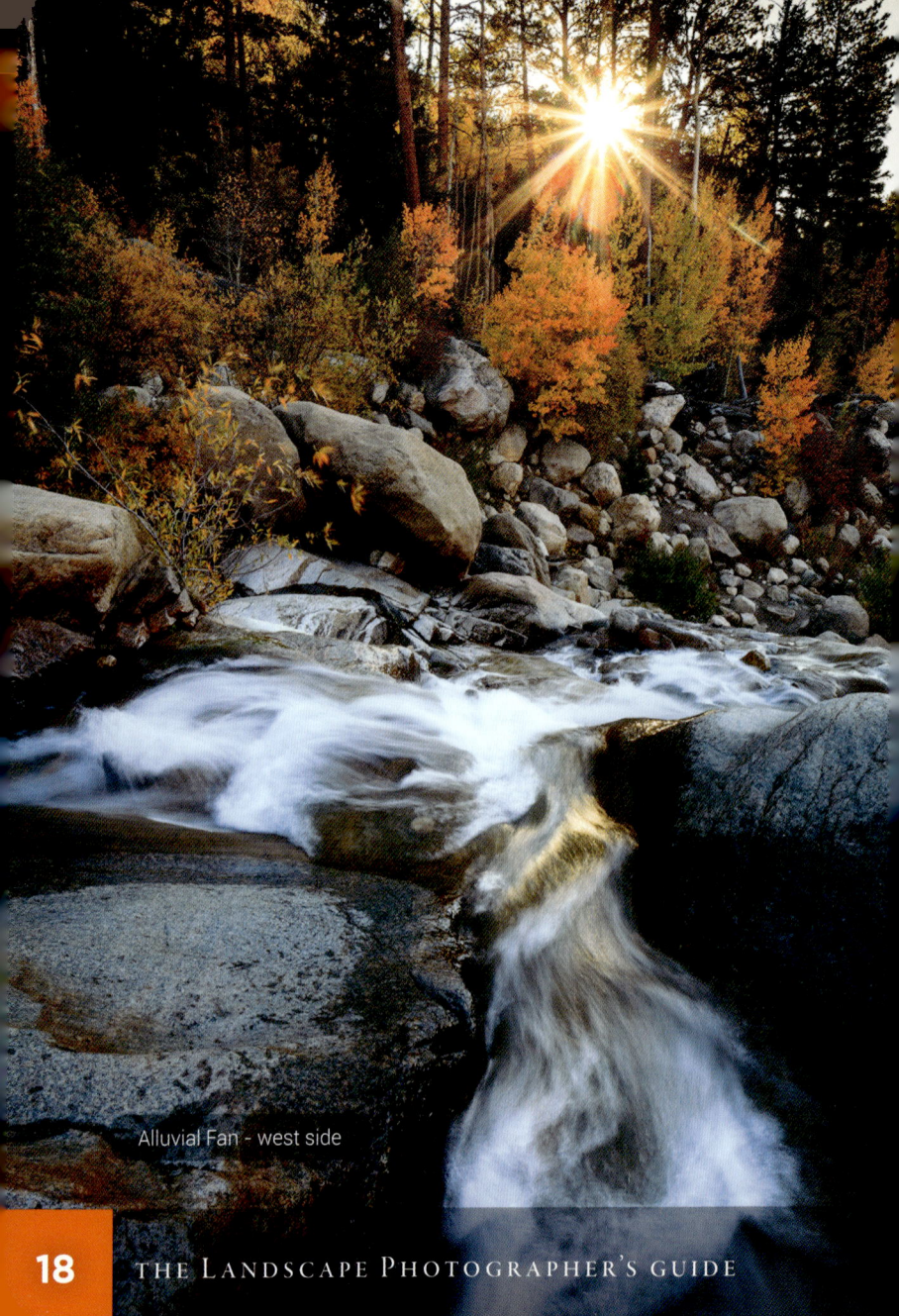

Alluvial Fan - west side

be stunning during the first week of October when the aspen trees glow with almost unbelievable vibrancy. Alternatively look to the east at sunrise and capture spectacular sunrises from here with Deer Mountain silhouetted on the right side of the photo.

As the road makes its way up the hill to the east there is a pull-over on the north side of the road. From here you can get a good overview of Horseshoe Park with the Mummy Range towering above it. This is a particularly good location during the winter months when the sun is far enough south to light the range at sunrise.

ENDOVALLEY

The far west end of Horseshoe Park is known as the Endovalley, because it is located at the end of the valley. There are several nice areas to shoot along here.

The Alluvial Fan is the first place you should stop. There are two parking areas—an east and a west. Both of these will provide different perspectives. The Alluvial Fan is a beautiful cascade that tumbles over large granite boulders that were deposited there during two major floods. It began with the Lawn Lake Flood in 1982 when a large dam about six miles up the river broke, flooding the entire area and significantly changing the landscape. In 2013

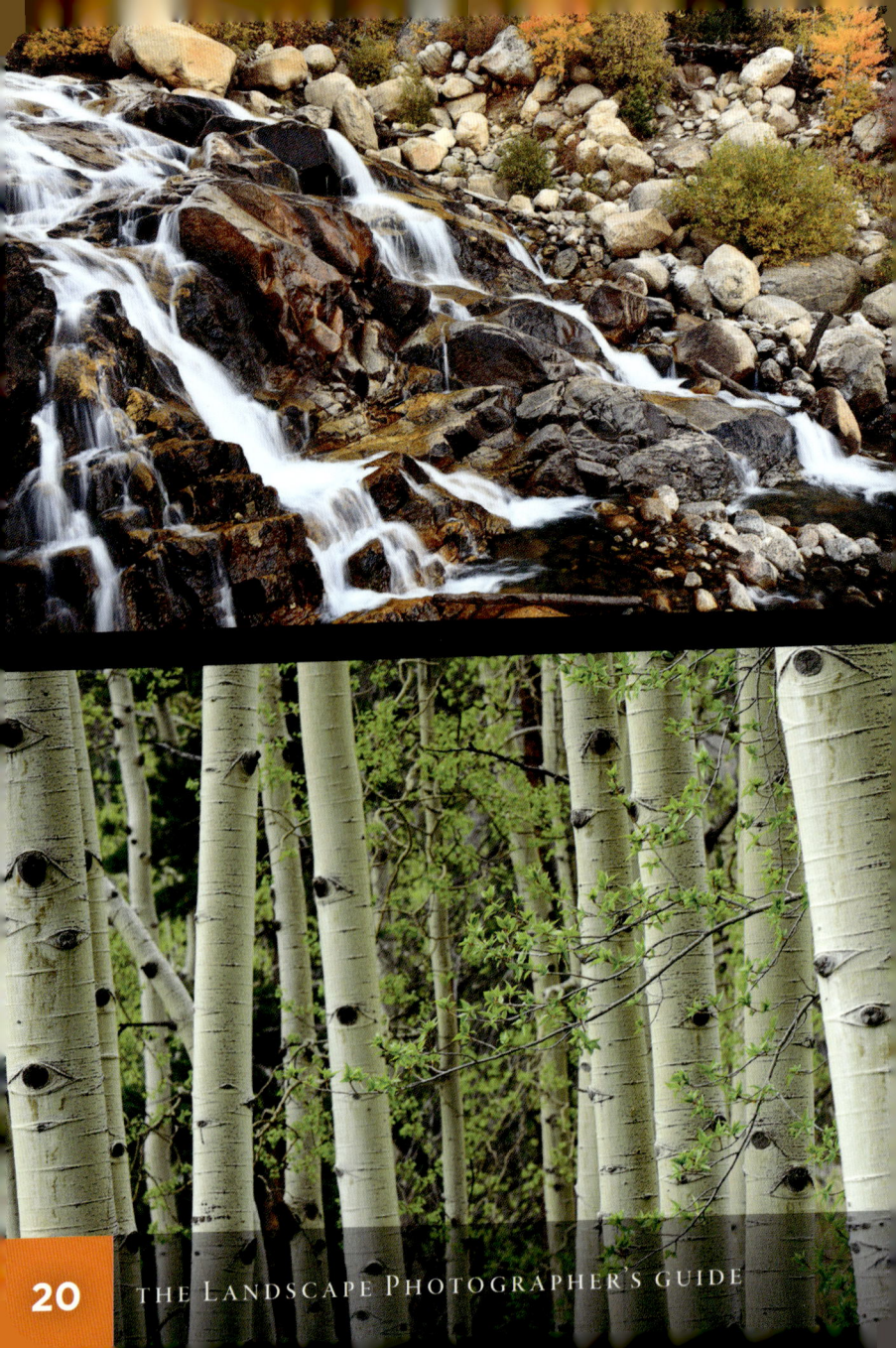

another major flood washed out the road and redirected the river.

The cascades afford a great number of compositional possibilities. Try getting in close to photograph one section and then back off to get the larger scene. Like most waterfalls, it is best to shoot during heavily overcast weather.

The next location in the Endovalley begins just after the west parking lot for the Alluvial Fan. It is a half-mile stretch of road with small meadows and groves of aspen trees. You may find it best to park at the West Alluvial Fan parking lot and walk from there.

In the spring and autumn, this road comes to life with glowing aspens, but at any time of the year you can find some great photos among the aspen forests along the side of the road. The unique texture on the aspen trunks is scarring from elk grazing on their sweet bark. It creates a nice repetitive pattern. The best stands can be found on the south side of the road.

You can also create images with the road leading the eye up to the mountains above. Include a few people or animals walking down the road for a sense of scale.

OLD FALL RIVER ROAD

At the very west end of Horseshoe Park, at the end of the Endovalley, Fall River Road turns into a one-way dirt road that begins its steep climb up to the Alpine Visitor Center, high above tree line. Once you start driving on this road, you need to go all the way up. You can expect it to take about an hour to get to the top. Along the way, there are several photo opportunities to be found. This road normally opens in early July.

The first place to stop is Chasm Falls, located about a mile and a half up the dirt road. This beautiful waterfall is twenty-five feet high and located in a deep, rocky channel of Fall River. It can't be viewed from the road, so you will need to park at the parking area and walk a minute or two down the steep trail to get a good view. It is best shot on either an overcast day or early evening after the sun has gone behind the mountains.

Continue up Fall River Road for quite a few miles until the trees begin to give way on the left side, revealing beautiful rugged views. In the early summer you can often find a lovely little waterfall descending hundreds of feet down the backside of Sundance Mountain. If you stop to photograph it, make sure you first find a proper parking place and then walk back to it so you don't block traffic.

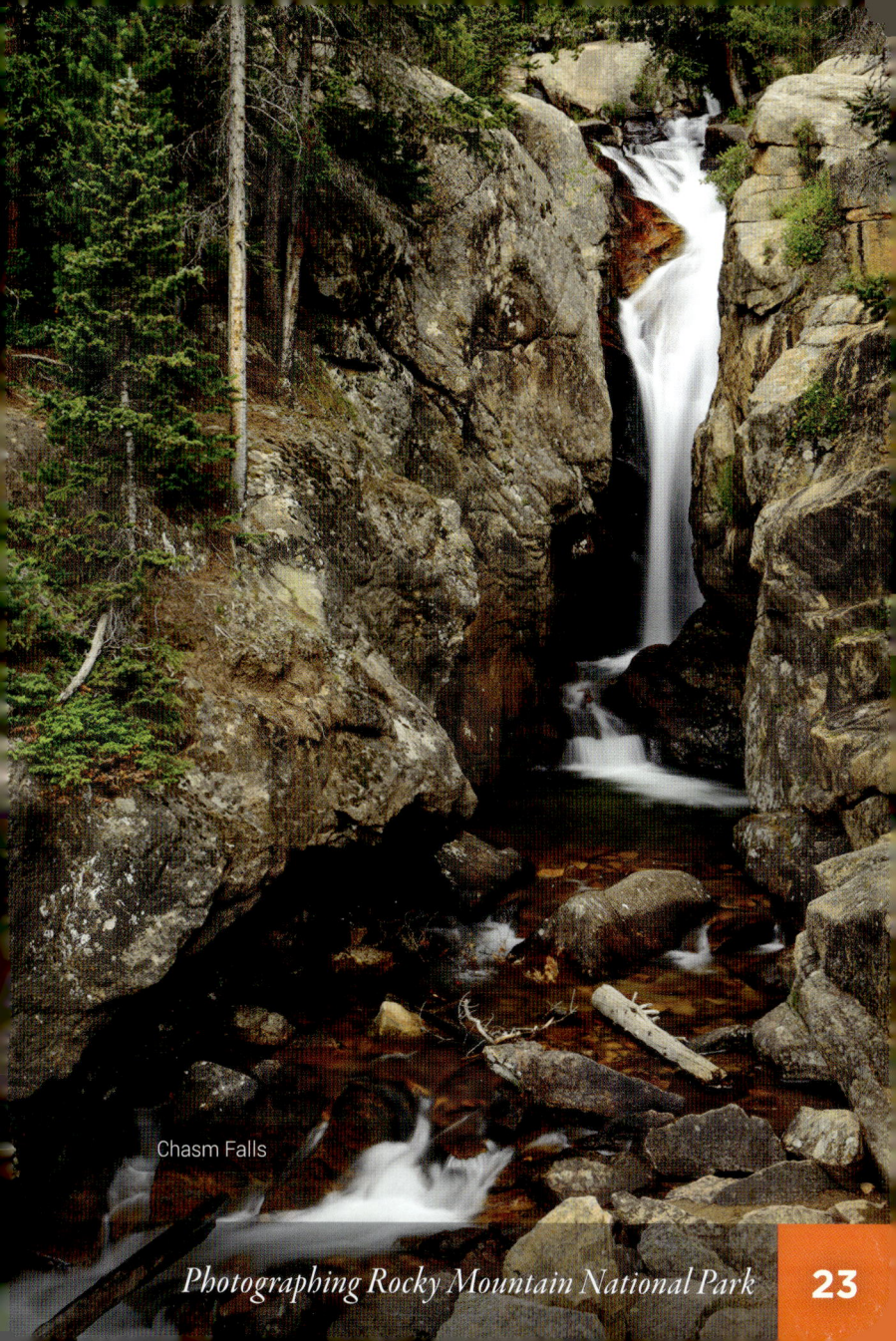

Chasm Falls

Once you finally get above tree line, there will be a number of gorgeous views on your left side. Just before the final ascent to the Alpine Visitor Center, you should notice a small pond just off the side of the road. It is located next to a trailhead for Marmot Point. This pond can be a nice place to photograph about forty minutes before sunset. You'll need to shoot from a low angle to avoid including the road. After shooting the pond, hike up to Marmot Point for spectacular tundra views in all directions. This is a nice spot from which to photograph the last light on the backside of the Mummy Range. Alternatively, there are some sunrise options here, using a long lens looking toward the west.

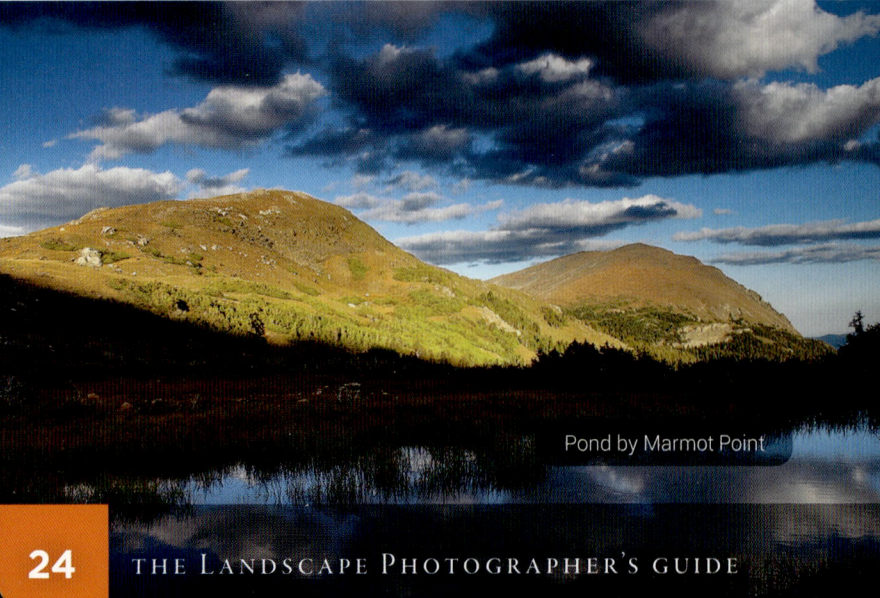

Pond by Marmot Point

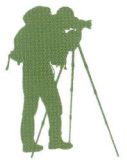

BEAR LAKE ROAD

To quickly get a taste of the best that Rocky Mountain National Park has to offer, take a trip down Bear Lake Road and visit some of the stunning locations that can be found just beyond this well-traveled tarmac.

MORAINE PARK

As you enter the park from the east side and pass through the Beaver Meadows Entrance Station, take the first left turn, which is Bear Lake Road. Less than a mile down this road you will arrive at Moraine Park. This stunning meadow was made to be photographed. The Big Thompson River winds its way through a lush meadow, which is often filled with elk, while the snowy peaks of the Continental Divide keep watch from above. If you want an easy-to-reach and beautiful scene, you will be hard-pressed to find anywhere better than Moraine Park.

My favorite location to photograph is alongside the river in the early morning. If you drive down Bear Lake Road to the south end of the meadow, you will find a parking area next to a bridge. Stop here and walk through the gate in the fence. Right next to the river is a classic shot with large stones in the foreground. Alternatively, follow the trail as it leads through the enclosure and then out alongside the river. Here and all along the trail you will find other photogenic options.

Another popular place from which to shoot Moraine Park is the museum, which sits on a hill on the east side of the meadow. From the museum parking lot you can capture the entire valley. If there is fog, you definitely want to head here to stay above it. From here you can also photograph to the south and include Longs Peak towering over the meadow.

You can also take the road opposite the museum and head west toward the campground. Along the way, there are several places with nice views over the meadow. These are particularly good places to shoot in early October when there is autumn foliage on this side of the meadow.

Please be aware that from September 1 through

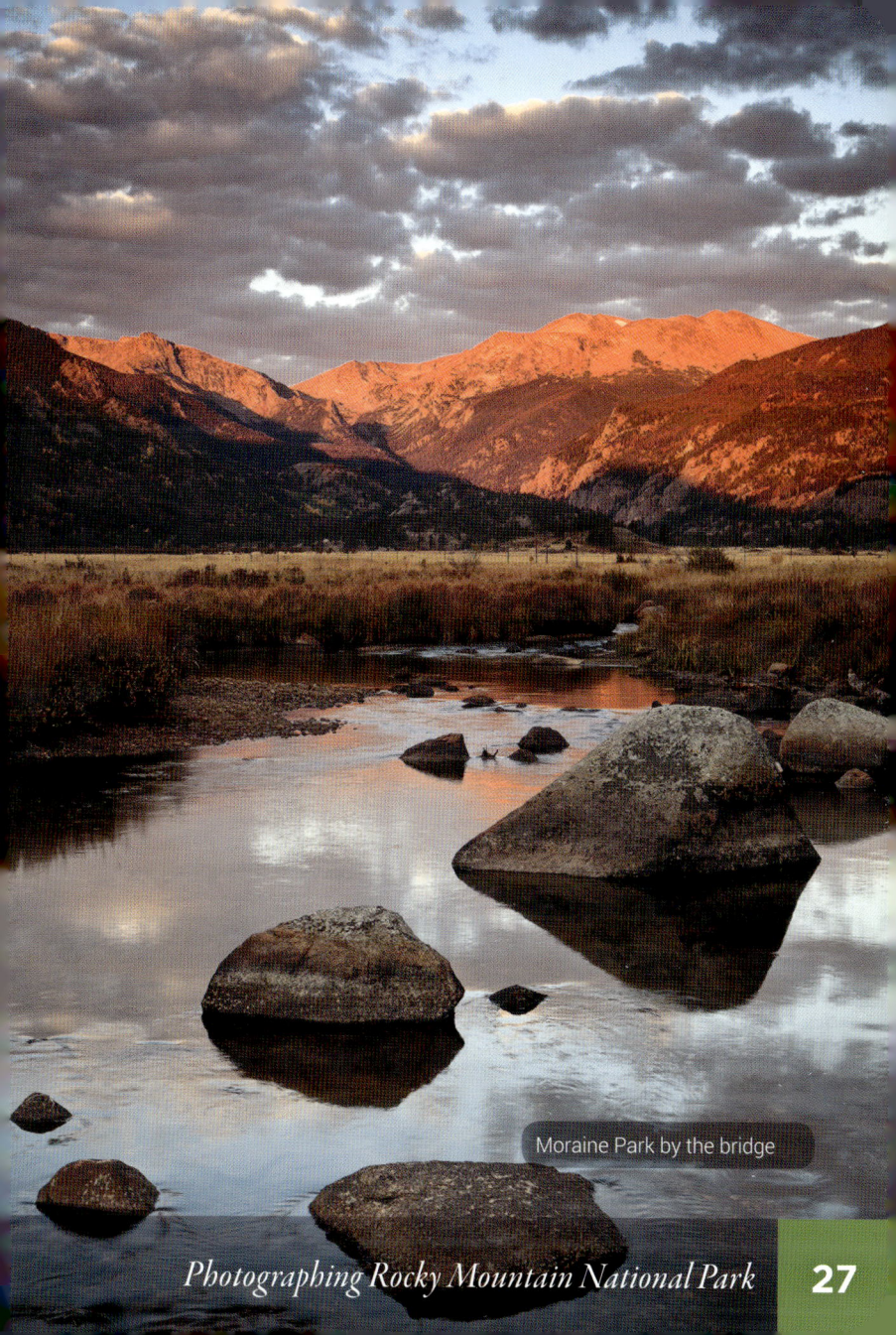

Moraine Park by the bridge

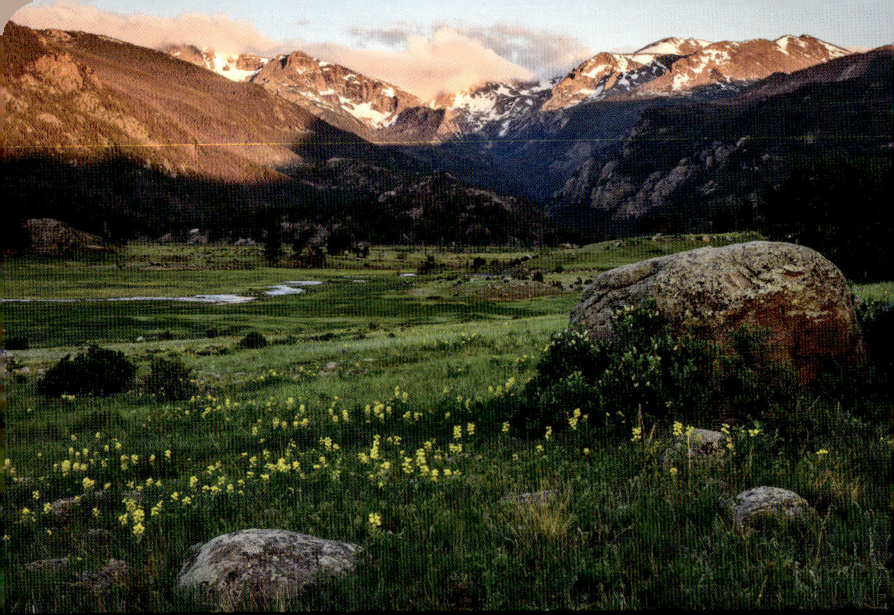

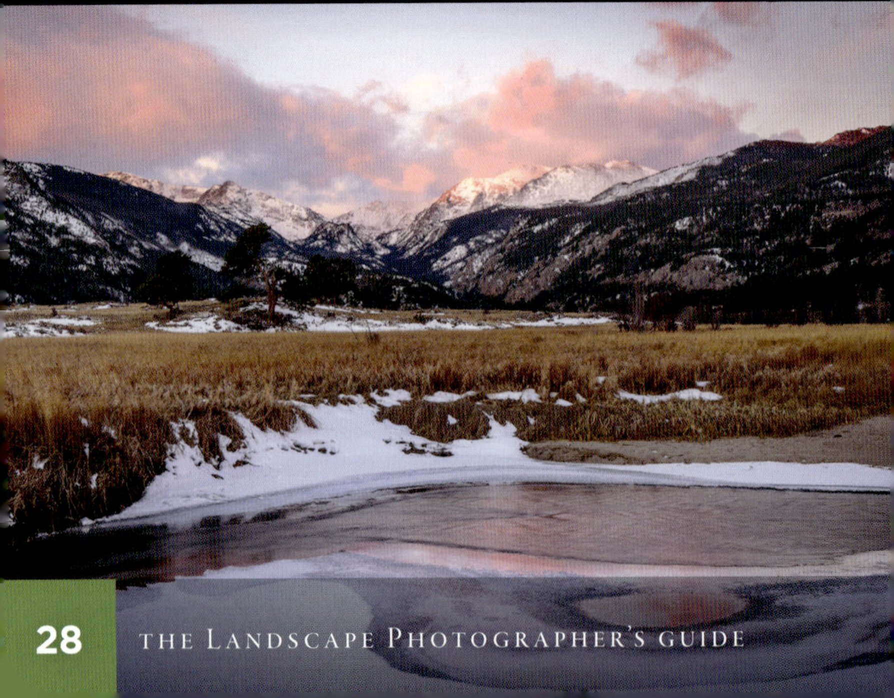

October 31, the meadow is closed from 5 p.m. to 7 a.m. to give space to the elk throughout the rut. During these times, you can still stand at the edge of the meadows and get terrific images. Over the years I've taken many great photos right from the side of the road in this area.

Moraine Park is one of those places that can be photographed all year long. Like most of Rocky Mountain National Park, it is best captured at sunrise or shortly thereafter.

CUB LAKE

Cub Lake is a 2.5-mile hike (one-way distance) from Moraine Park, and so may not be for everyone. However, it is a fairly gentle hike compared to many other hikes in Rocky Mountain National Park and brings you through a number of different environments. The trail begins at the west end of Moraine Park. Follow the road that begins just opposite the museum until you reach the Cub Lake parking area.

Right at the beginning of the trail, two small bridges cross the Big Thompson River. Walk to the east of the second bridge to photograph it with the Continental Divide in the background. In this area you can also find a great variety of wildflowers during the summer. Focus on getting close-ups of these, but be sure to shoot them from the trail so as not to damage the surrounding meadow.

Continue on the trail and it will bring you along the edge of Moraine Park where you might see elk grazing just off to the side. The trail then reaches Cub Creek and heads west through a beautiful forest. Along the way, you will see beaver ponds and large ponderosa trees, as well as streams and meadows. You never know what wildlife you'll find on this stretch.

Eventually the trail begins its upward climb, taking you through a beautiful aspen forest, which is especially brilliant in the spring and autumn. There are limitless abstract photos to be found along this section of the trail. After the aspen forest, you are almost at Cub Lake.

The first thing you may notice when you arrive is that a fire moved through the area in 2012 as a result of an illegal campfire. The area is healing, but it will be many years before it is fully recovered. Fortunately, there are many flowers to photograph. In the summer months lily pads with their big yellow flowers cover the lake. If you continue on the trail past the lake, you will soon find yourself walking through thick patches of brilliant fireweed. This can be a good area to photograph life returning after a fire.

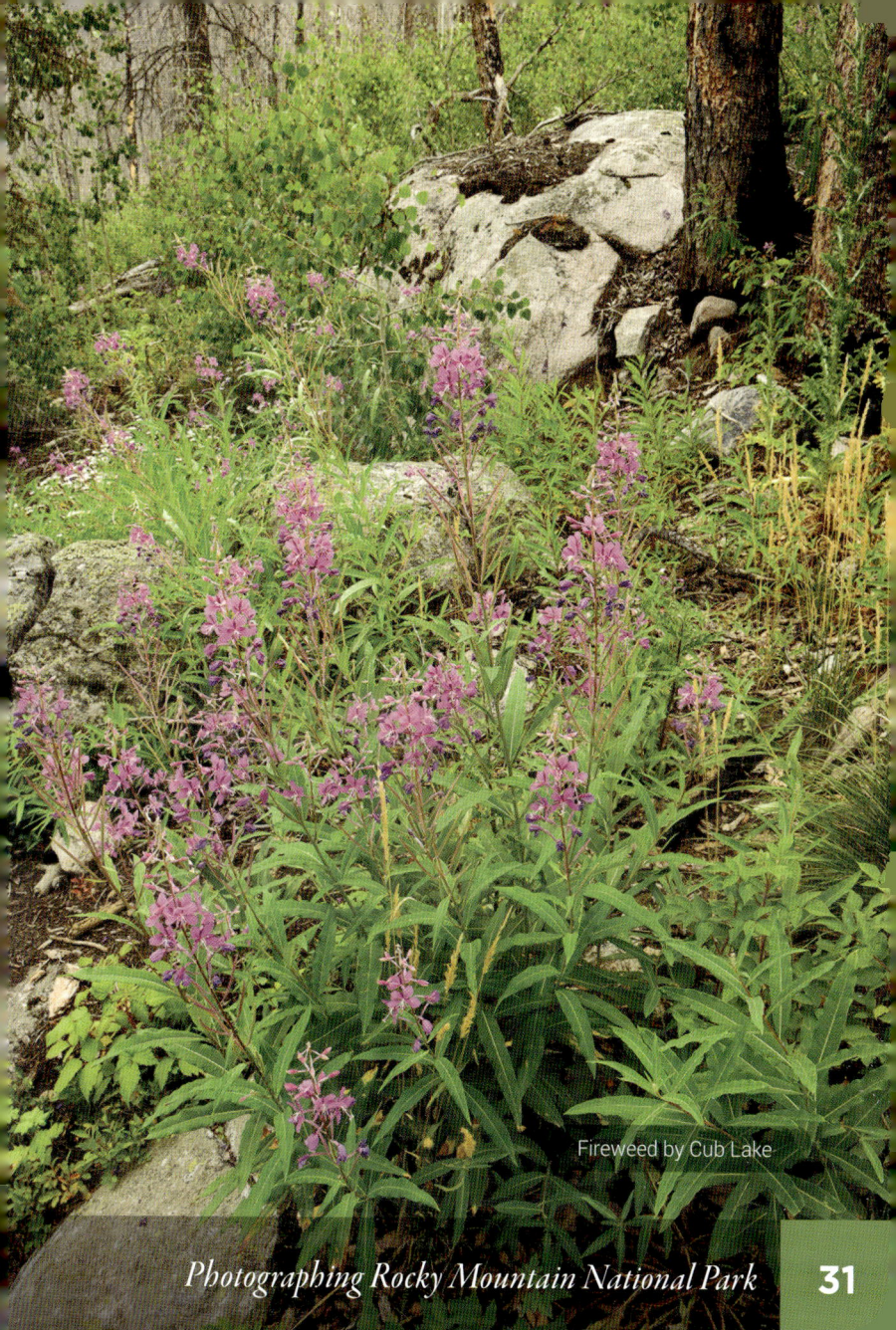

Fireweed by Cub Lake

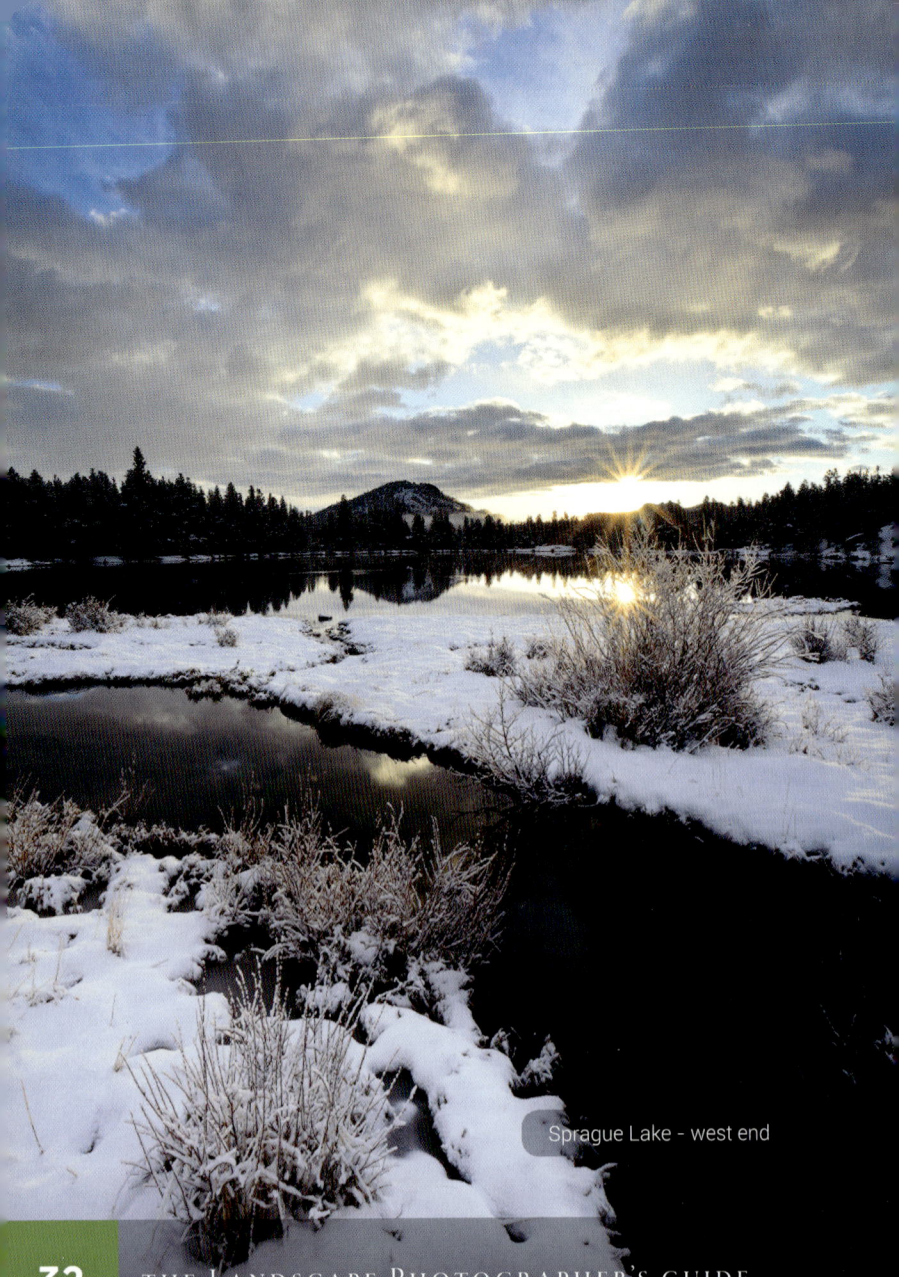

Sprague Lake - west end

SPRAGUE LAKE

One of the most iconic views of Rocky Mountain National Park can be seen at Sprague Lake. This beautiful artificial lake was created by Abner Sprague, one of the early settlers to the region, to support his lodging activities. It couldn't have been placed in a more stunning location. It is one of the easiest places to visit in the park, as you can drive right to it from Bear Lake Road and then follow an accessible trail all the way around the lake.

The primary location for photographing the lake is from its far-eastern end. From here you have an unobstructed view of the Continental Divide, and on calm days the reflection in the water is magical. There are also a few stones in the water you can use as interesting foreground elements.

About a third of the way around on the north side of the lake, just a little east of the stream, there are also some good views looking toward the Continental Divide. If there are a lot of photographers at the main location, then this is a good alternative location.

In certain conditions—such as when the mountains are hidden by clouds, when there is a lot of color in the eastern sky, or when you want to capture the sun rising above the trees—you will want to photograph from the bridge on the southwest side of the lake. You can often get a good

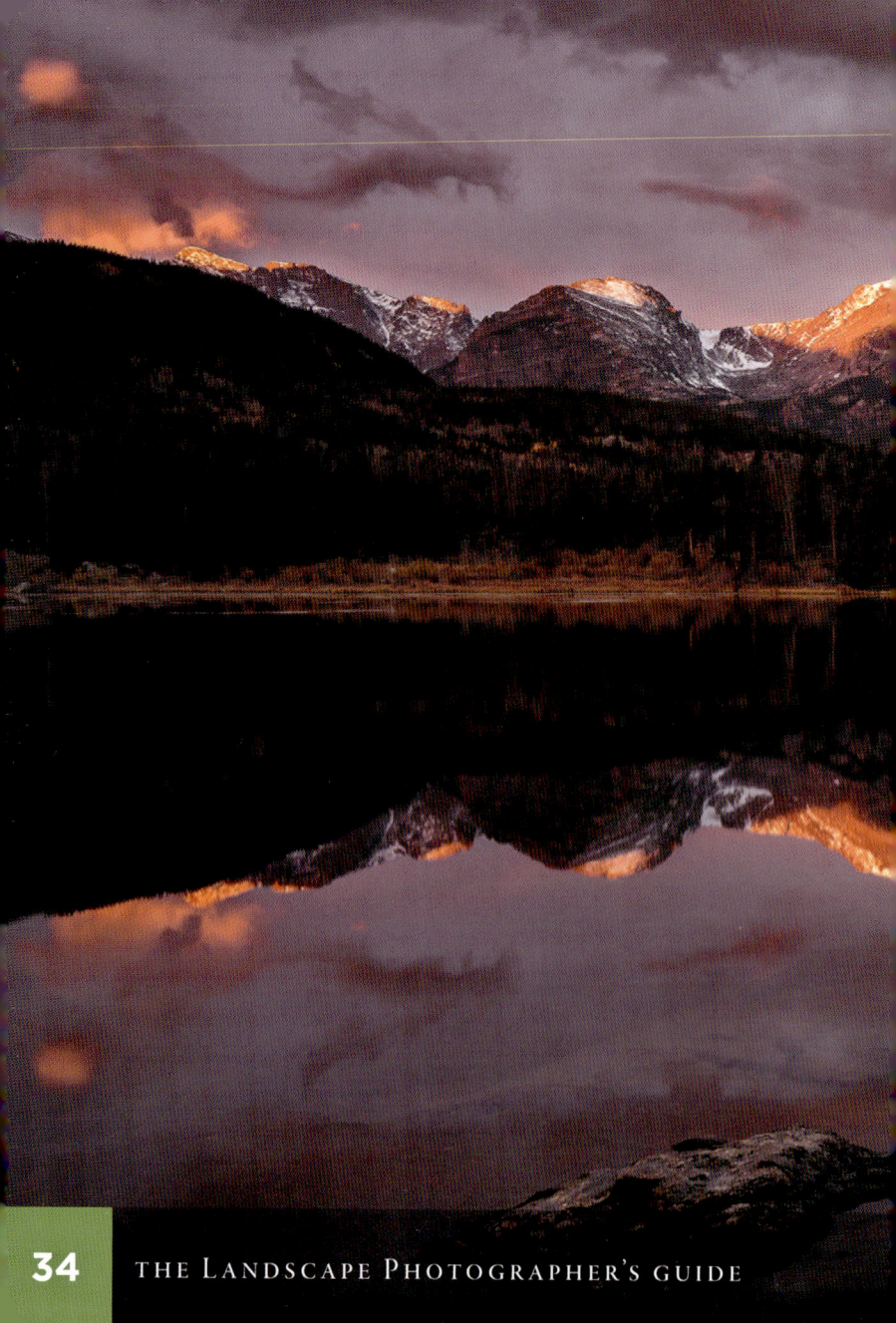

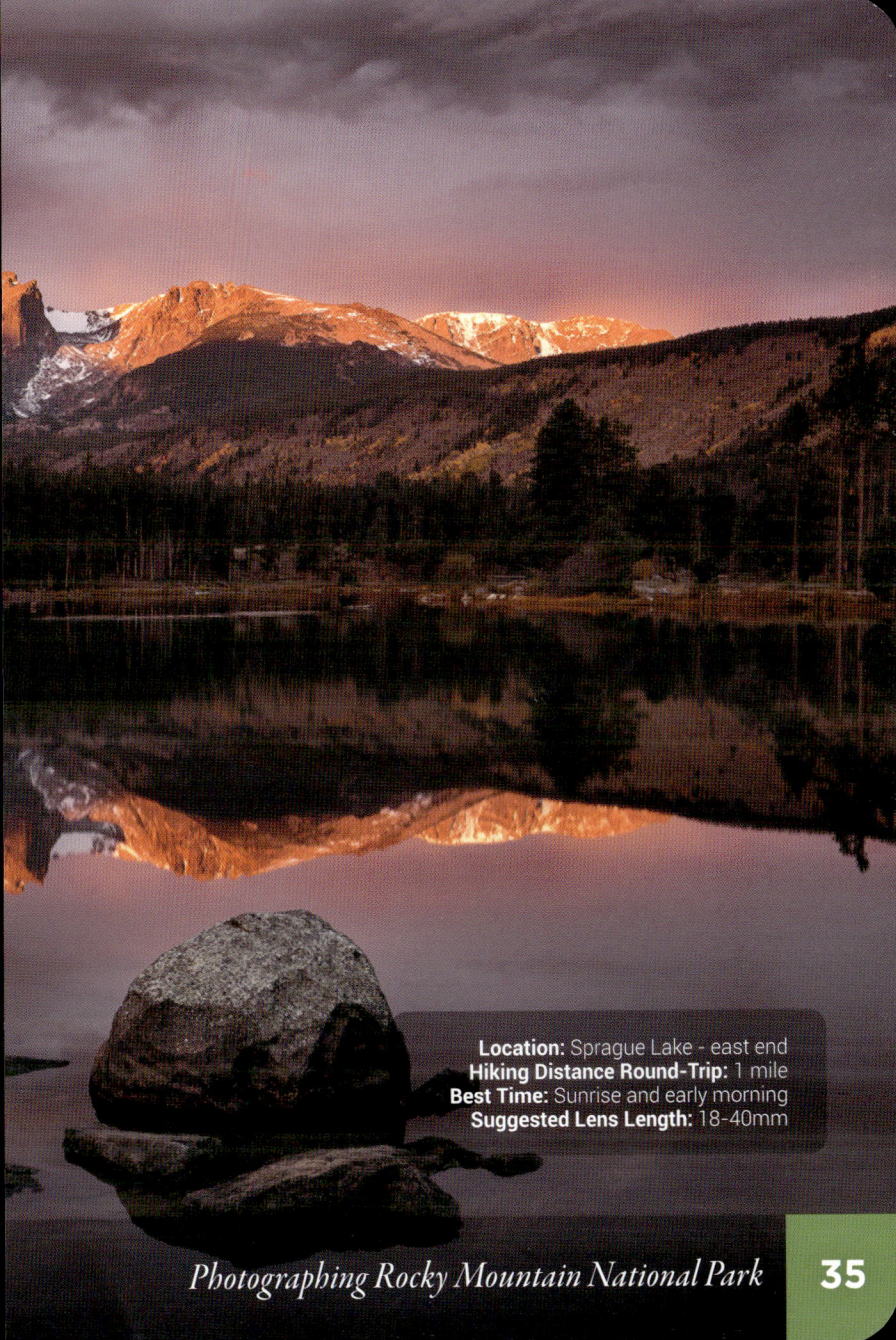

Location: Sprague Lake - east end
Hiking Distance Round-Trip: 1 mile
Best Time: Sunrise and early morning
Suggested Lens Length: 18-40mm

Photographing Rocky Mountain National Park

reflection in the smaller patches of water among the grasses next to the bridge.

This lake is such a peaceful place during the early morning that, even if you don't have good conditions for photography, it's worth the effort. It is not uncommon on summer mornings to find elk playing in the water or even moose celebrating the start of the day. Even if you can't get a good photo on the day you go, just sit and enjoy the sounds, smells, and sights.

STORM PASS TRAILHEAD

Just before you reach the Bierstadt Lake Trailhead, there is a small and discreet parking area on the left side of the road with just four parking spaces. It may not look like much, but this area provides a wonderful view of the Continental Divide with almost no effort required. Make sure to stop here and take a look.

When you get out of your vehicle, follow the trail heading to the west and you will see Taylor, Otis, Hallett, and Flattop peaks all looking down on this little meadow. At sunrise they take on a brilliant glow.

In the fall, this is one of the best places to enjoy the autumn colors. Generally, the best time to be here is the last week of September or the first week of October.

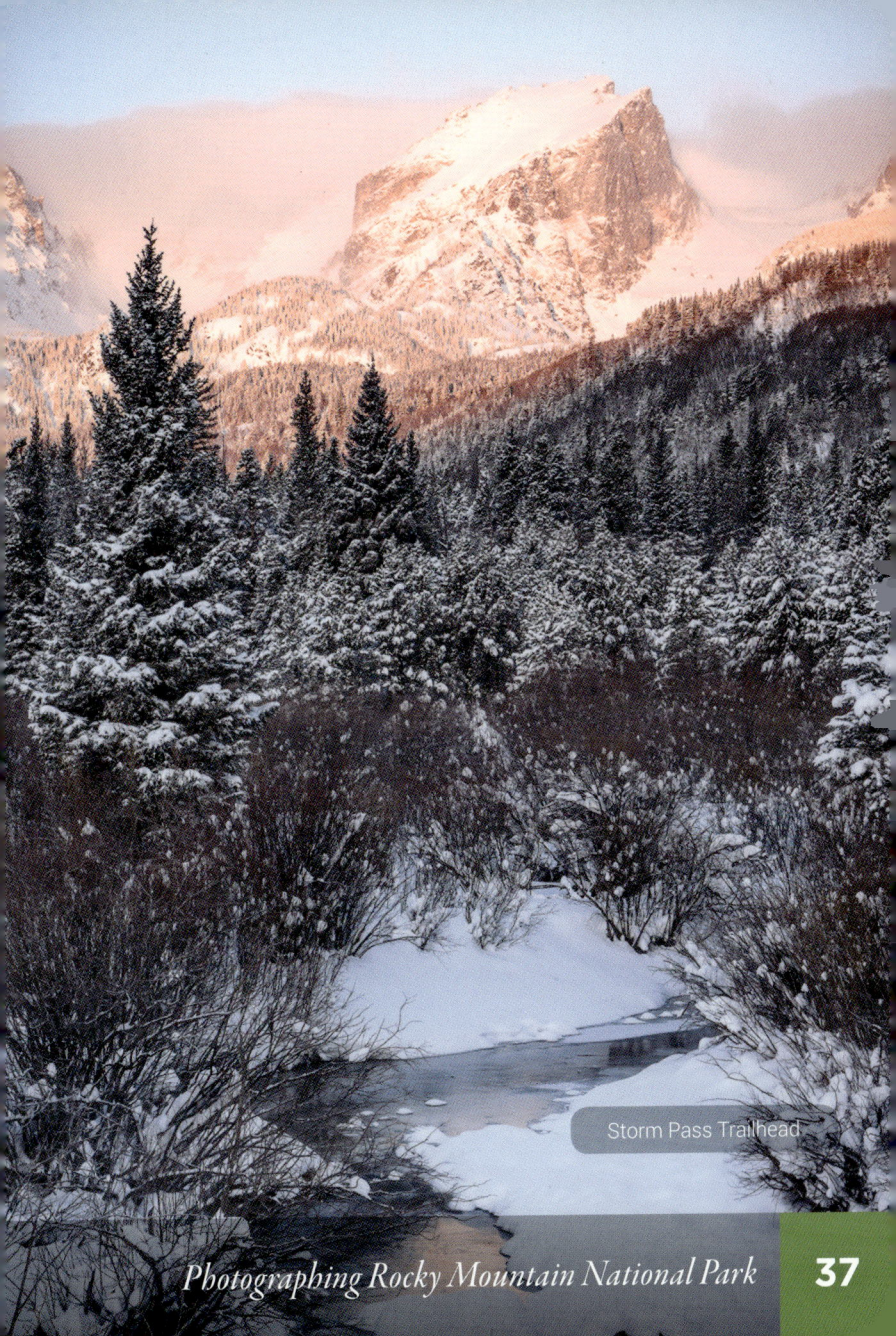

Storm Pass Trailhead

Photographing Rocky Mountain National Park   **37**

The entire Bierstadt Moraine glows in shades of yellow and orange and provides many beautiful photographic opportunities. In the summer, there are often wildflowers growing in this meadow, so you can try getting down low to include the flowers in this scene.

BIERSTADT LAKE

This lake was named after Albert Bierstadt, the famous artist of the early 1900s whose dramatic paintings helped inspire the preservation of many of the natural wonders of the United States, including Rocky Mountain National Park. He visited this lake and was inspired by the stunning views it affords.

There are two ways to reach Bierstadt Lake. The shorter approach is from the Bierstadt Trailhead located on Bear Lake Road. From here, the trail winds up twelve switchbacks, climbing about 500 feet in elevation. You'll need to be fairly fit to take this approach. The distance from this trailhead to the best photographic vantage point is about a mile and a half, but give yourself extra time, as the elevation gain will have you breathing hard. Alternatively, you can begin at Bear Lake. The trail begins on the northeast corner of Bear Lake. It begins with a bit of an uphill climb but then levels off. It is definitely gentler, but it's a

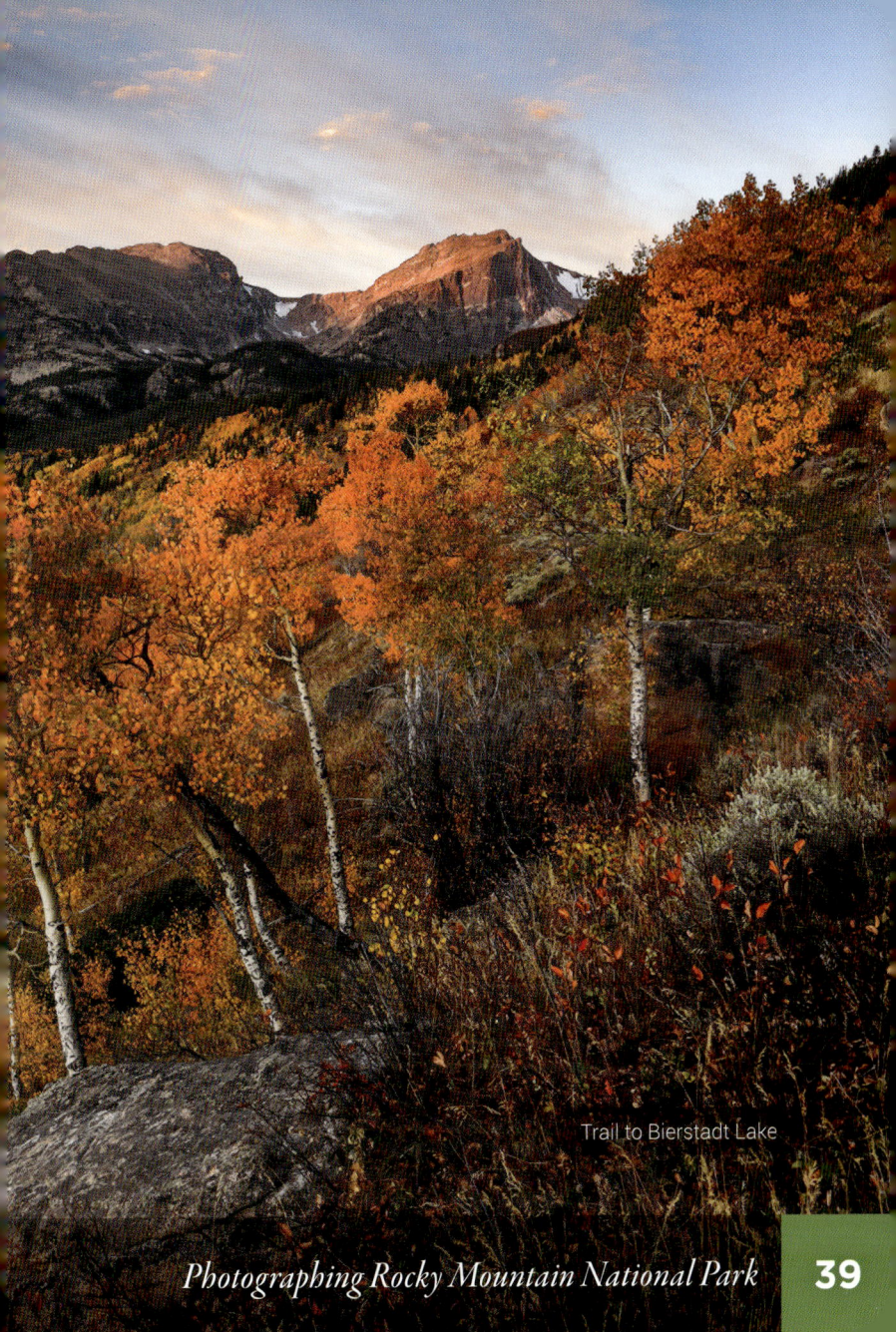

Trail to Bierstadt Lake

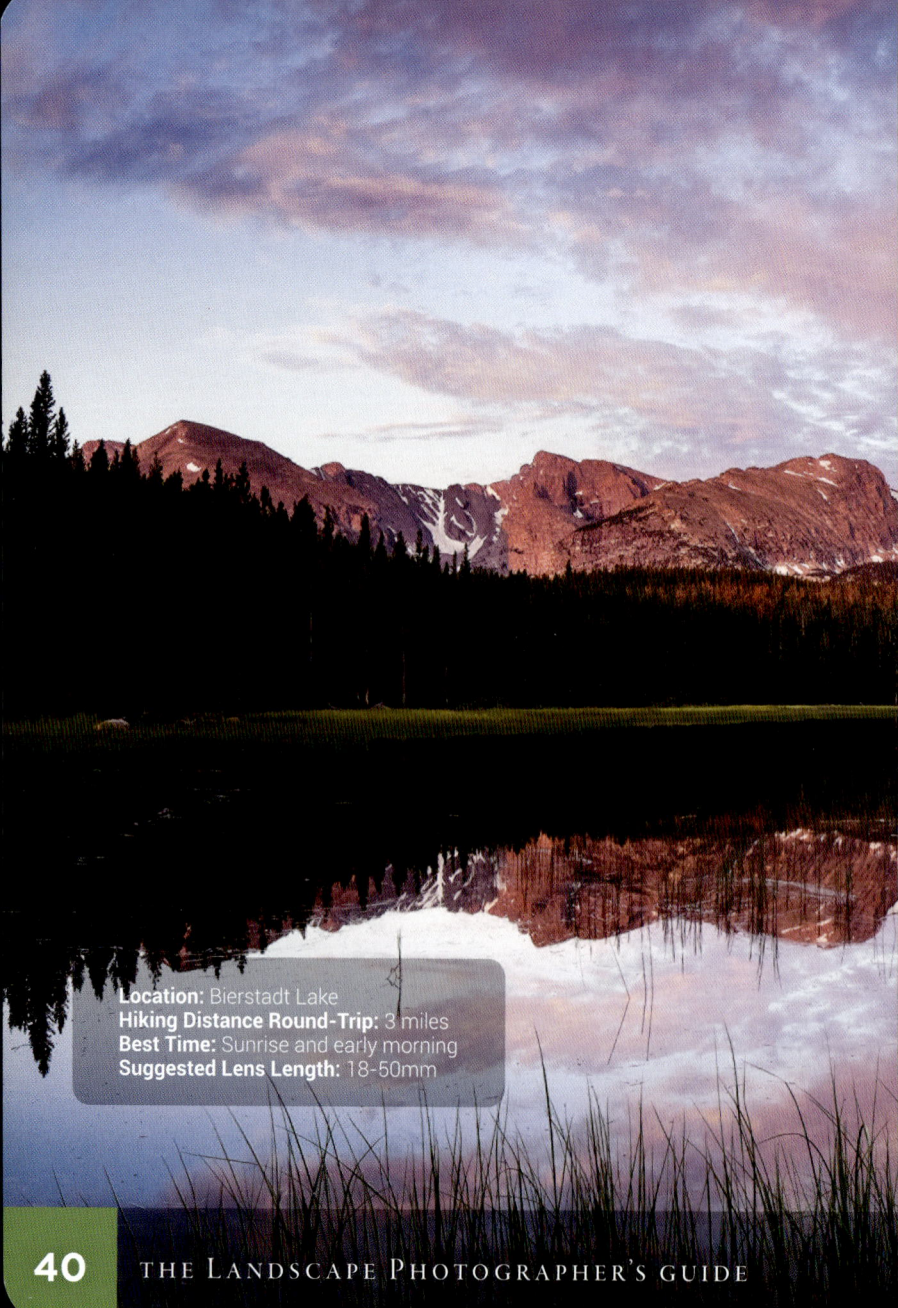

Location: Bierstadt Lake
Hiking Distance Round-Trip: 3 miles
Best Time: Sunrise and early morning
Suggested Lens Length: 18-50mm

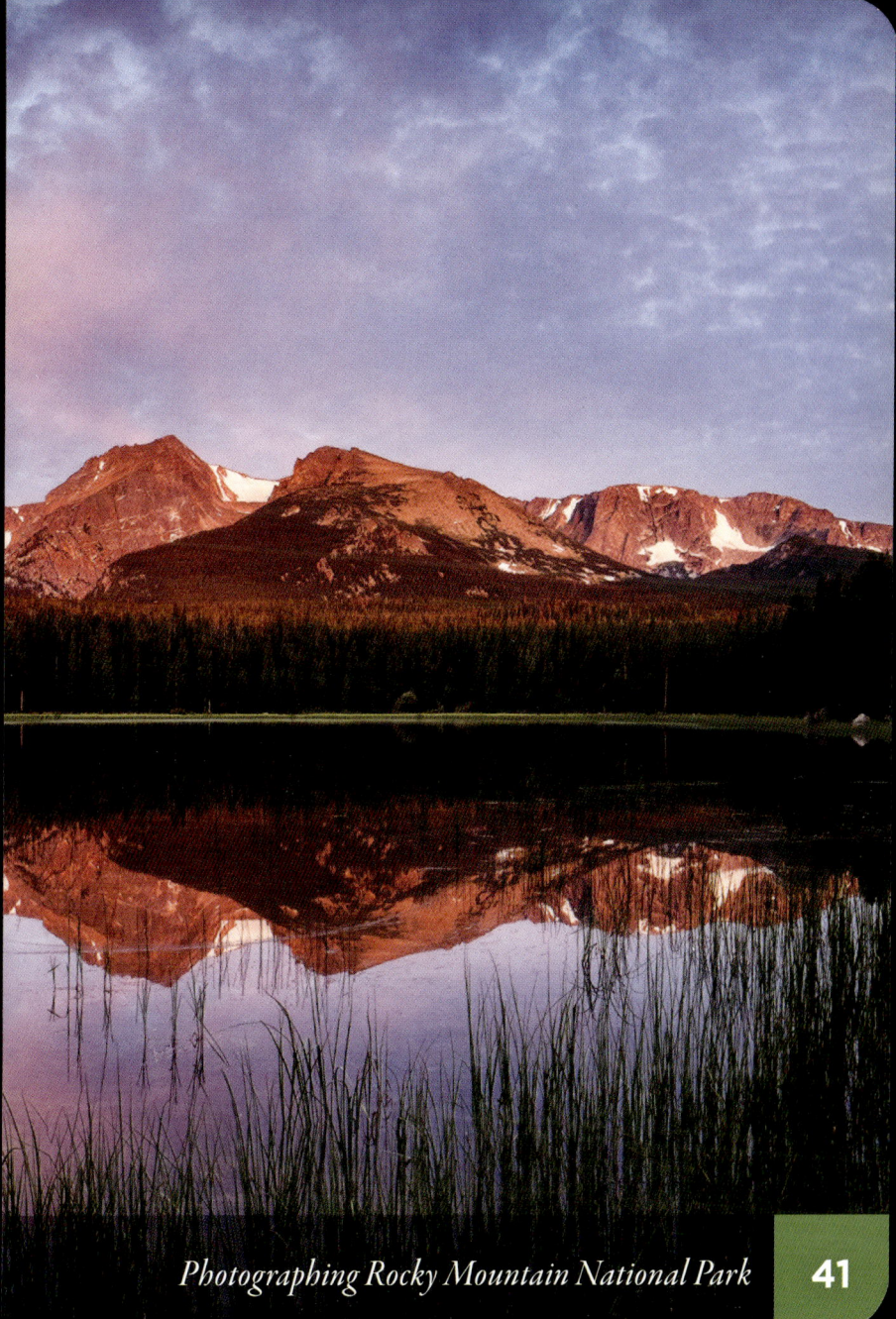

mile longer than the other trail each way, so make sure you begin early enough.

Upon reaching Bierstadt Lake from either trail, follow the forested trail all the way around to its eastern end. You will know you've reached the eastern end of the lake when you come to a bridge with a small stream. This is the outlet stream from the lake. Follow the trail next to the stream up to the lake and you will find yourself on a sandy beach with impressive views of the Continental Divide.

The photographic options from here are pretty obvious. The mountains tower over the west side of the lake and on calm days cast their inspiring reflection on the water. In the summer, grasses grow on the edge of the lake that can be used to provide some foreground interest.

If you parked at the Bierstadt Trailhead on Bear Lake Road, then you will find some other nice options as you descend the switchbacks. There are some spectacular views into Glacier Gorge from here. In the autumn, you will be surrounded by golden aspen trees, which make a great foreground.

ALBERTA FALLS

About one and a half miles past the Bierstadt Trailhead is the Glacier Gorge Trailhead. This trail leads to many wonderful places in the park, such as Mills Lake, the Loch, Sky Pond, and Black Lake. Along the trail to these locations, your first stop will likely be Alberta Falls.

Alberta Falls is probably the most visited waterfall in Rocky Mountain National Park. It is a small waterfall—about twenty-five feet high. While there are other more spectacular waterfalls in the park, this one is probably the most accessible and has its own unique character.

The walk to the falls is just under a mile each way and provides some delightful views along the trail. The trail begins at the Glacier Gorge Trailhead, where it heads down into a small meadow often filled with flowers in June. It then descends to cross a rushing stream. The trail then climbs a steep slope. At the top, it enters a forest of young aspens. This stretch is magical when the trees are at their peak autumn color around the last week of September. This area can be a great place to photograph people as they walk down the tree-lined path. After about ten more minutes of walking, the trail then joins Glacier Creek, passing several small photogenic cascades before arriving at Alberta Falls.

There are a number of different ways to photograph these falls. You can include the aspen tree beside it, which can be very nice in the spring and autumn when the colors

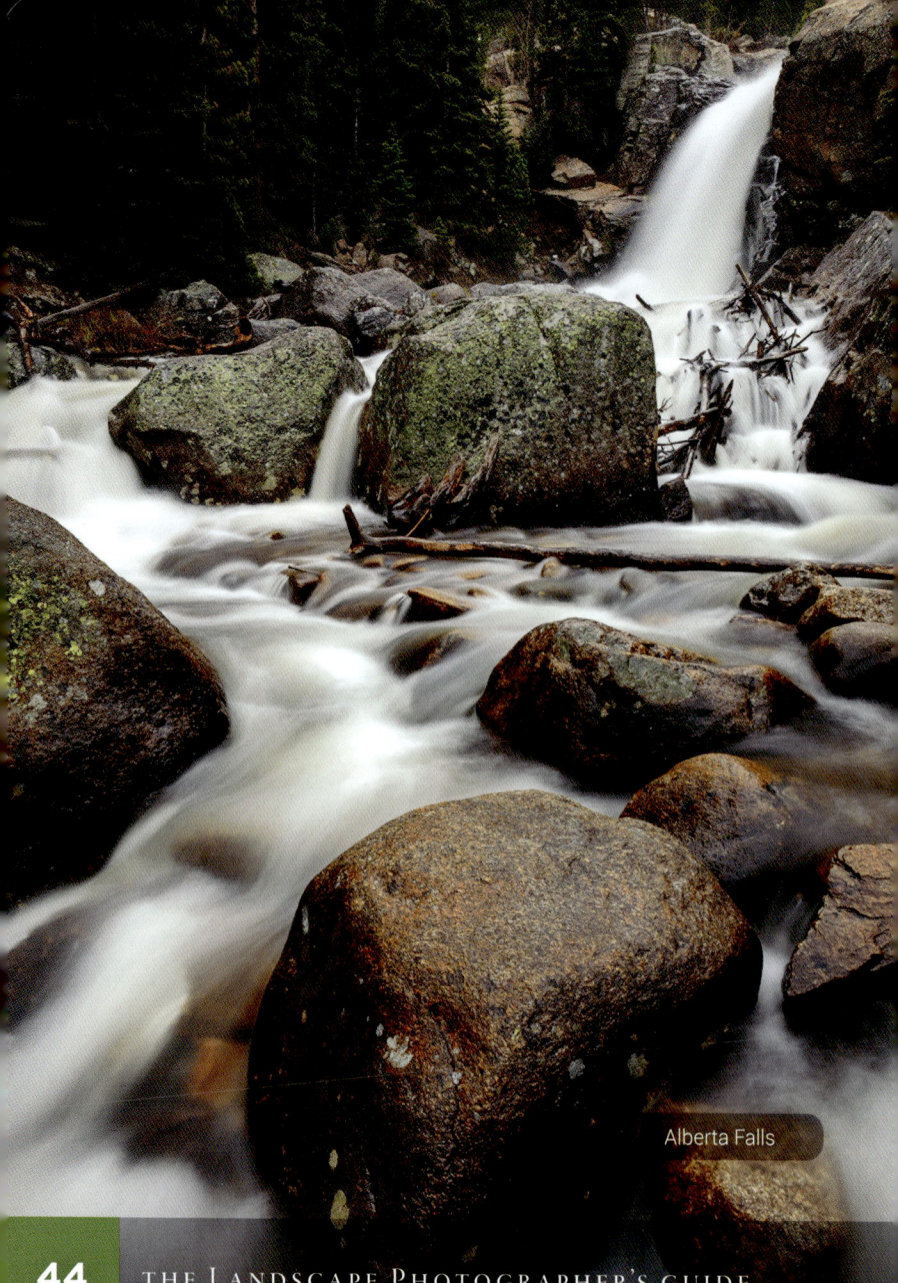

Alberta Falls

are vibrant, or you can get down low near the stream to give the image more depth. Don't try this during a heavy spring flow, as that would be very dangerous. Generally, I avoid including the sky when shooting these falls; it is usually so much brighter that it ends up being distracting.

Alberta Falls, like other waterfalls, is best photographed when there is no direct sunlight on it. Ideally, you should photograph waterfalls on days when it is heavily overcast, especially if you want to create a gentle feel to the waterfall. Remember that in the spring there is generally a very strong flow, and in the autumn there is much less water running through. The change in water flow will give a different feel to each image and will require a different shutter speed.

When shooting waterfalls, I always use a tripod and a slower shutter speed. Generally, I switch my camera to shutter speed priority, which means that the camera will adjust your aperture to give you the right exposure while maintaining the shutter speed you have set. I start with a shutter speed of about one-third of a second (0.3") and then adjust from there to get the feel I want.

MILLS LAKE

Mills Lake is one of the most beautiful lakes in the area

and is named after Enos Mills, the "Father of Rocky Mountain National Park," who did more than anyone to help create RMNP. This lake just oozes drama and beauty.

The trail for Mills Lake begins at the Glacier Gorge parking lot on Bear Lake Road. It is a roughly three-mile hike each way and makes for a great half-day outing. Make sure to bring enough food, water, and appropriate clothing for changing weather.

Mills Lake is very popular with hikers and photographers, but it is one of the more challenging lakes to photograph well. The main reason that Mills Lake is difficult to photograph is that it runs from north to south and is surrounded on the east and west by steep peaks. The result is that the lake gets neither good sunrise light nor good sunset light, so one must be content with midday light, which is often less than flattering to an image. Yet if you visit I'm sure you will agree with me that it is well worth photographing.

The best place from which to photograph this lake is from the first point the trail lets you down to the lake. Here a rock outcropping lets you out over the water. Just to your south you will find a couple of interestingly shaped trees and a large precariously balanced boulder. These make great foreground images as you capture

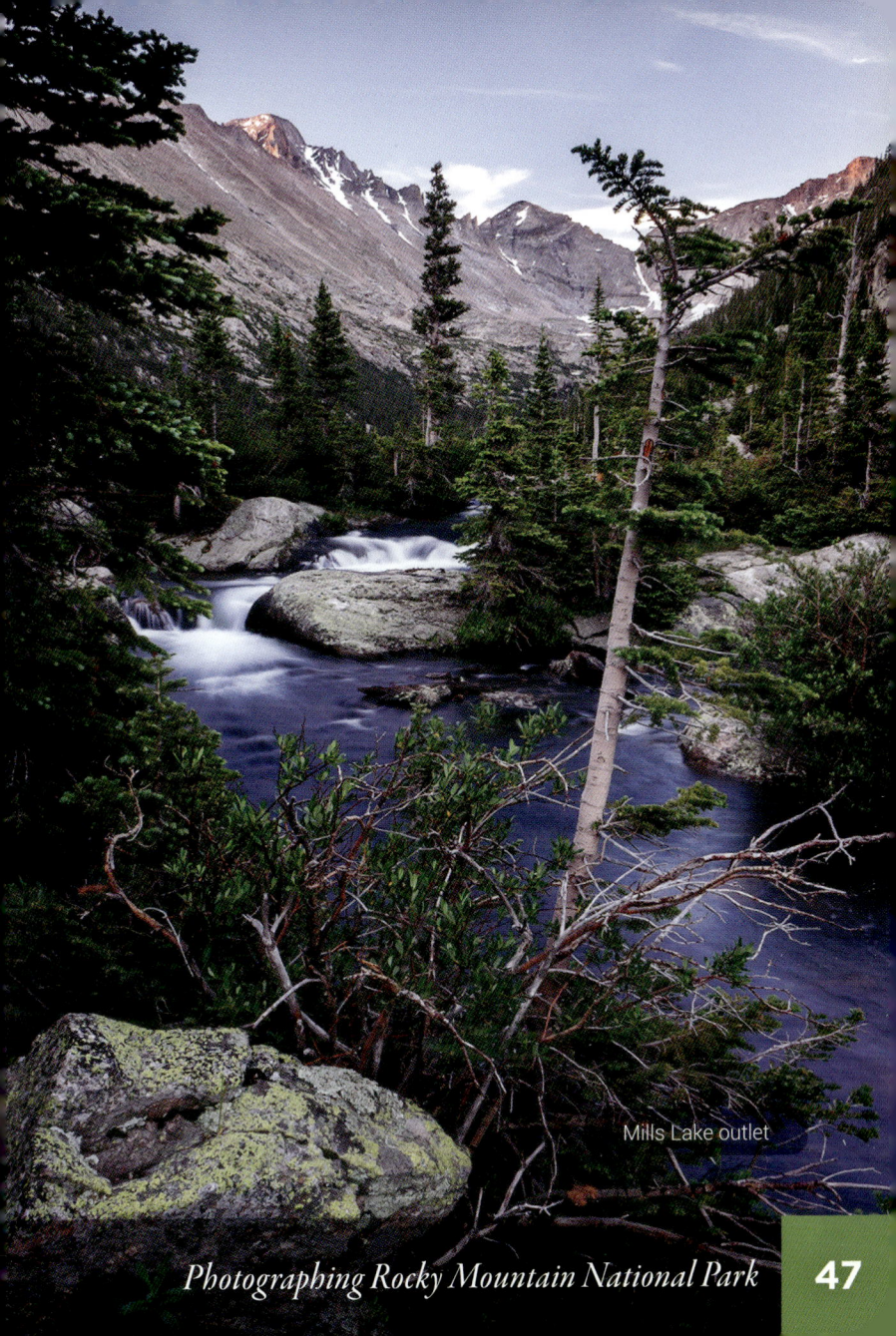

Mills Lake outlet

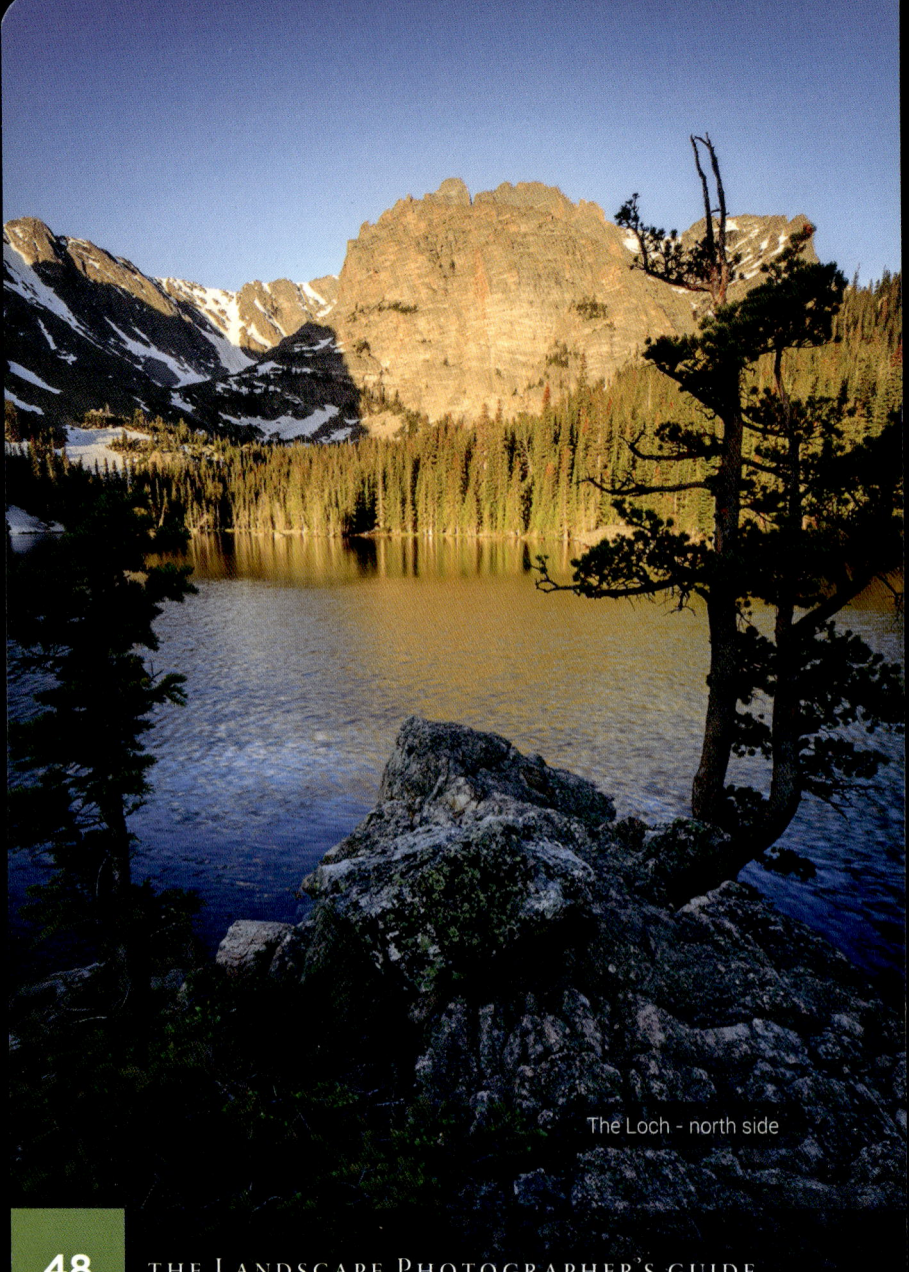

The Loch - north side

Longs Peak, Pagoda, and Chiefs Head looking down from above. On calm days the reflections to be found here are beyond tranquil.

THE LOCH

The hike to the Loch also begins at the Glacier Gorge parking lot. The hike is roughly three miles (six miles round trip) and has 1,000 feet of elevation gain. You need to be fairly fit to hike up here but you won't regret the effort. The Loch was actually named after a Kansas businessman named Locke in the early days of the park, though *Loch*, the Scottish word for "lake," was used instead.

This lake lies on a shelf just over 10,000 feet high. It is ringed by lodgepole pine with jagged peaks soaring above it. On the far side of the lake stands a gorgeous rock face known as the Cathedral Wall. I assume it was given this name because of the way its spires and imposing form convey a sense of awe. If you arrive in time for sunrise you'll be awed by the way it glows with the day's first light.

Just as the trail meets the lake, you will find one of the best compositions. It is a little bay on the lake with a narrow channel leading to the larger part of the lake. This narrowing of the shoreline creates a natural frame for the sides of the image, and rocks in the water add interest to the foreground.

Along the northern shore there are several places where you can incorporate the interesting trees and rocks in the photo to give it a greater sense of place. If you continue along the northern shore you eventually come to a small meadow on the left-hand side, which is right on the lake. This is a nice spot from which to shoot if the water on the lake is calm, as it can provide a perfect reflection of the Cathedral.

The Loch is a great destination any time of year, including winter. To get the best photograph you will want to be here just prior to sunrise, which will mean an early start from the trailhead.

If you have energy, you can continue up the trail another mile to Timberline Falls, one of Rocky's more impressive waterfalls. It has several different tiers and the trail actually runs right up alongside it. If you pay attention, you can see and hear it from the Loch.

Beyond Timberline Falls, you will find even more wonderful areas. Just at the top of the waterfall is Lake of Glass, which is rarely as still as its name implies. About another half mile beyond this lake is one of the real gems of Rocky Mountain National Park: Sky Pond. Many consider this to be one of their favorite lakes in the park.

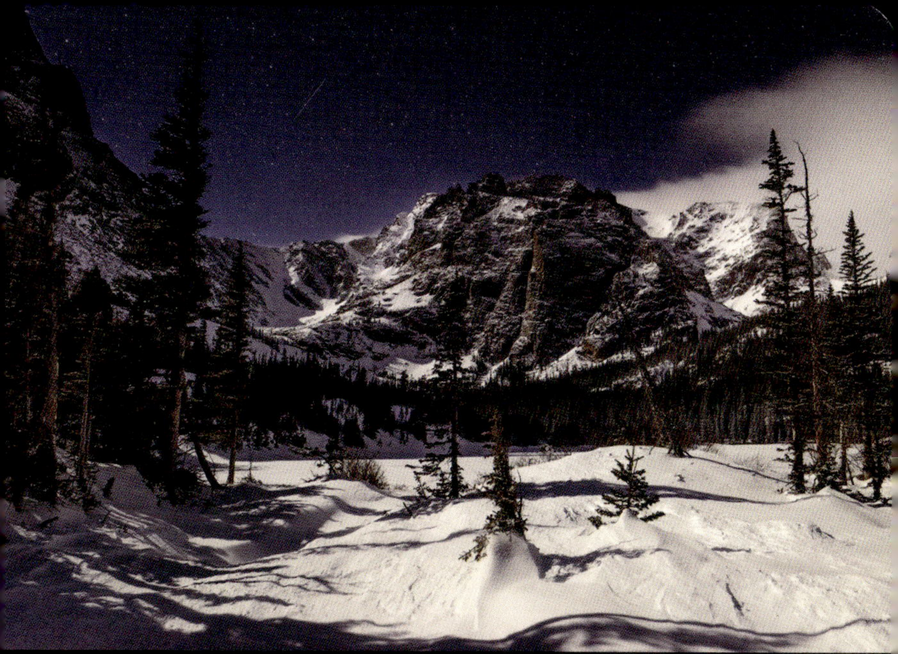

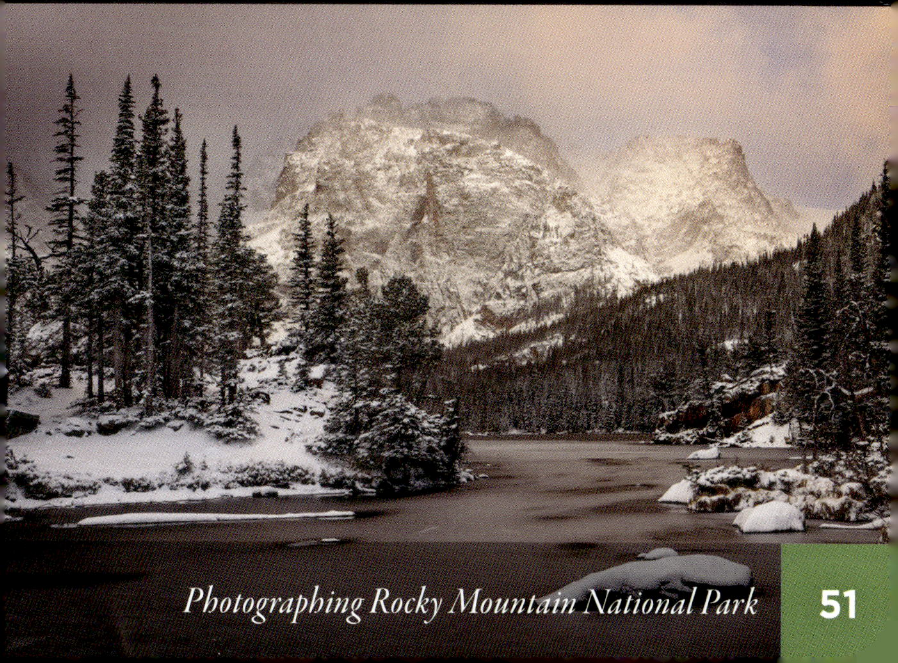

To really photograph this well, you need to be here by sunrise. You will also need a very wide-angle lens, as the granite spires rise right up from the lake.

BEAR LAKE

Bear Lake lies at the very end of Bear Lake Road. It is one of the most visited locations in Rocky Mountain National Park, and for good reason. This little lake is nestled in the forest near the base of Hallett Peak and Flattop Mountain. It is one of the few mountain lakes that can easily be reached by car, with only a short, flat walk from the parking lot. The trail around the lake is quite gentle and much of it is accessible.

The obvious view you see when you reach the lake is of Hallett Peak looking down on Bear Lake. This is not the best view to photograph. While you can occasionally get some nice shots looking toward Hallett Peak in the west, the best view is to be found on the north end of the lake by the large aspen-covered boulder field. From here you can look south across the lake and enjoy a clear view of Longs Peak, which is the highest mountain in the park.

The best time to photograph from the north side of Bear Lake is from late afternoon until just after sunset. Look for a day when there is no wind, as you will then find a beautiful reflection. A few clouds above Longs Peak can help to make your photo more interesting. Try to incorporate some of the lakeside rocks in the foreground of your photo.

In the autumn, many photographers climb the large boulder field on the north side of the lake to capture Longs Peak through the multicolored aspen trees. Scrambling up the boulders requires a fair bit of agility and can be very dangerous, so it is not recommended for most people. If you do climb up, there is a spot quite high up in this aspen grove where you can often get orange aspen trees on one side and yellow on the other side during the last week of September. In the mornings, these aspen trees light up nicely and almost seem electrified, but most of Longs Peak is in the shadows in the morning. In the evening, Longs Peak lights up but the aspens are in the shadows. Unfortunately, you can't have both at the same time.

As I mentioned above, Bear Lake is primarily a late-evening/sunset location but you can also try your hand here at sunrise. Look for a morning when clouds sit above Longs Peak but do not block the eastern horizon. Alternatively, head up the trail 1.1 mile to Dream Lake for an idyllic sunrise location.

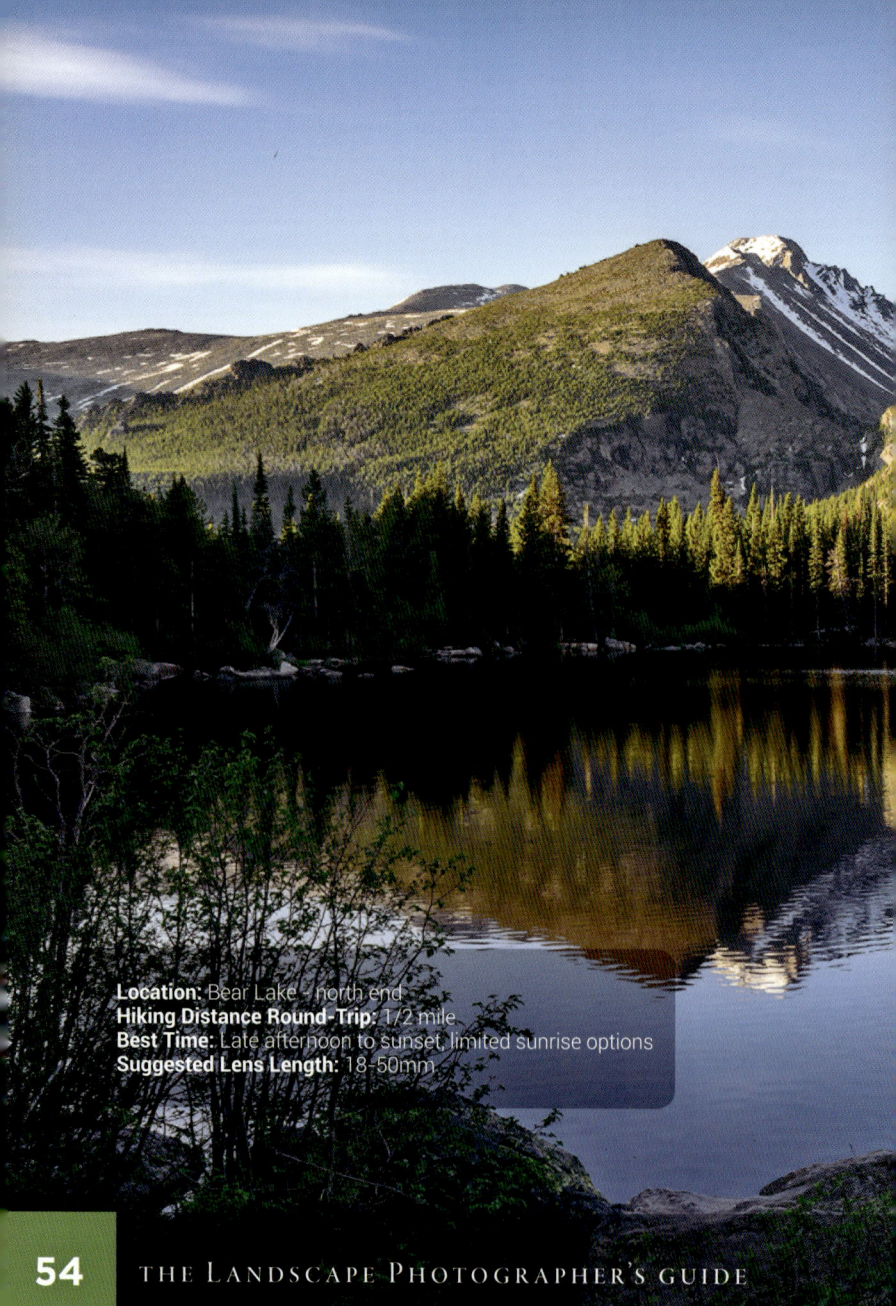

Location: Bear Lake – north end
Hiking Distance Round-Trip: 1/2 mile
Best Time: Late afternoon to sunset, limited sunrise options
Suggested Lens Length: 18-50mm

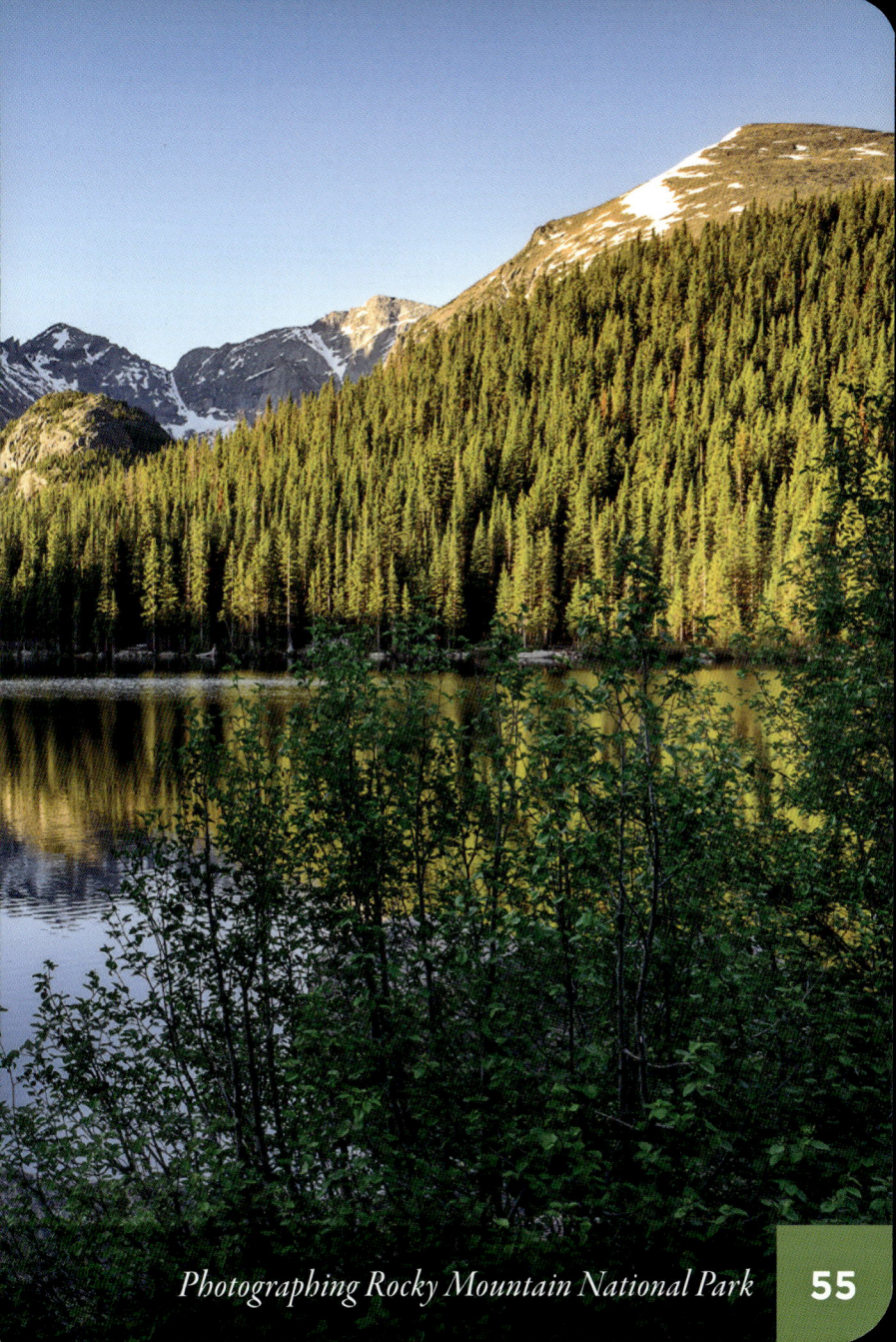

NYMPH LAKE

About halfway up the Dream Lake Trail you will find a small pond called Nymph Lake. This spot is often overlooked by photographers even though they hike right past it on their way to Dream Lake. There are some good photo opportunities to be found here if you know where to look.

In the morning you can photograph up toward Hallett Peak from the east shore down between the trees. Take care to walk carefully and to stand on rocks if at all possible. Also, make sure not to step in the grassy restoration area, as the Park Service are trying to allow that area to fully revegetate.

The better view, however, is found on the north shore during the evenings. Follow the trail around the lake until you see a spur trail leading down to a platform and bench on the north shore. From this spot you can look to the south and see a nicely composed view of Longs Peak. Since the water here is often still, you may be able to capture a nice reflection of the peak in the water.

If you continue up the trail toward Dream Lake you will find several additional great views of Longs Peak. These locations can be spectacular during the early evening and through sunset. This is an area you should put high on your list for evening shots.

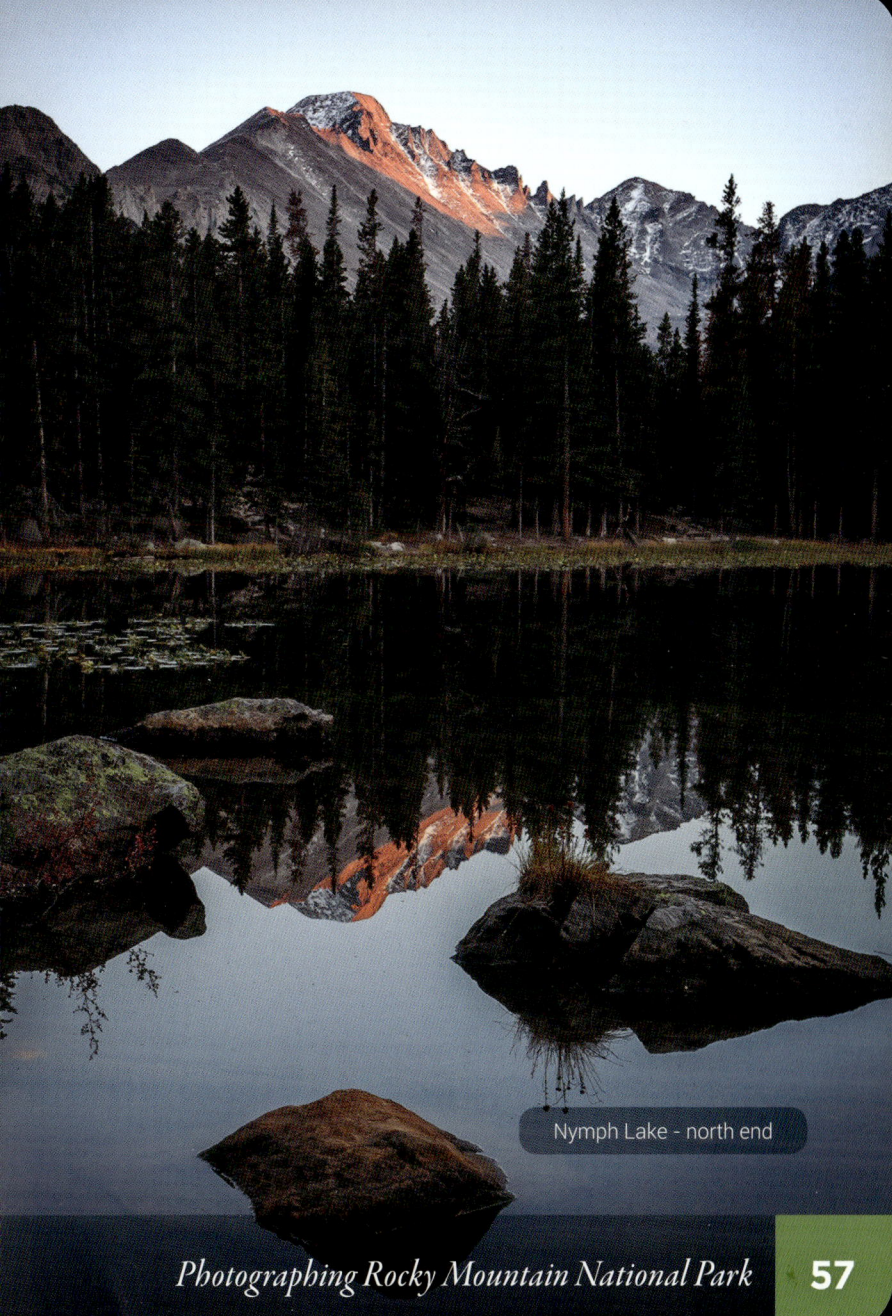

Nymph Lake - north end

DREAM LAKE

When photographers ask me where to shoot, the first place I usually suggest is Dream Lake. It simply begs to be photographed and is one of the iconic views of Rocky Mountain National Park. Dream Lake lies just below the towering granite walls of Hallett Peak and Flattop Mountain (which looks anything but flat from this angle). The lake stretches out toward the peaks, making your photos feel like you are being pulled into the scene.

Dream Lake is best photographed at sunrise, but you can still get some great images up until an hour or two after sunrise. It is one of those places that makes for great photos all year long. I personally prefer to be here just as the ice is forming or thawing on the lake in the autumn or spring, but any day can be a good day to photograph this lake.

You will find that certain areas around Dream Lake are off-limits; please respect these areas to allow them a chance to re-grow. Most of these areas can, however, be accessed in the winter and early spring when thick snow protects the fragile vegetation.

If you come up here in the winter to take advantage of this incredibly photographic lake, make sure you take the time to look down at your feet. The ice on the lake takes on amazing patterns and on a weekend during the winter you will often find several photographers crawling around on their hands and knees looking for the very best ice fractures to photograph.

The trail to Dream Lake begins just behind the ranger hut at Bear Lake at 9,475 feet elevation. It is a 1.1-mile hike (one-way distance) with a little over 400 feet of elevation gain. If you are not accustomed to the altitude, it would be wise to give yourself about an hour to get there from the trailhead.

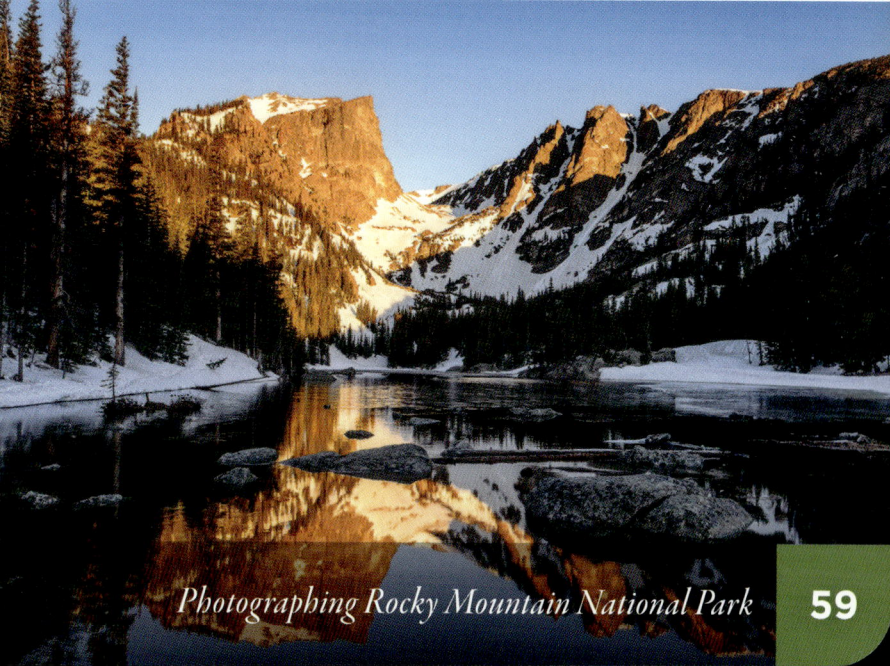

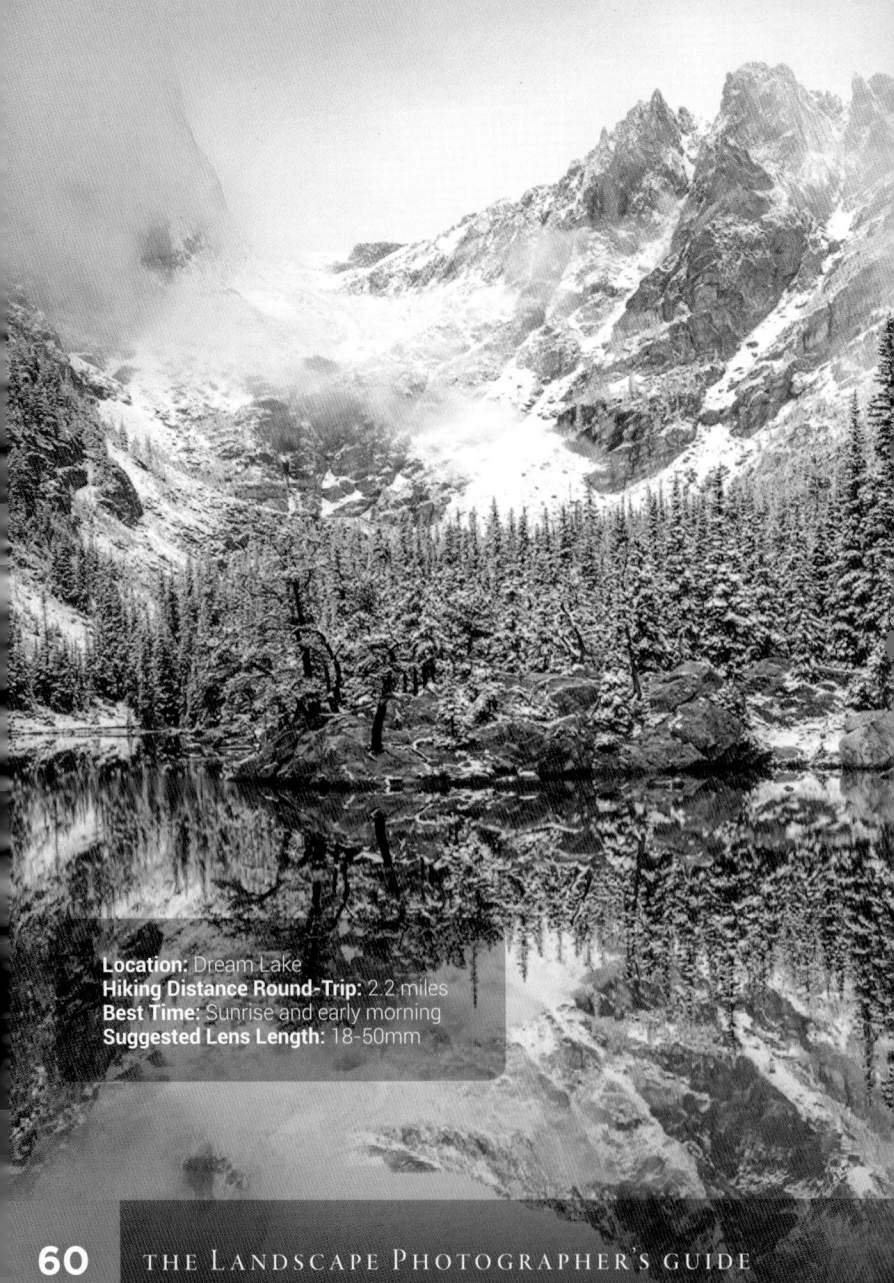

Location: Dream Lake
Hiking Distance Round-Trip: 2.2 miles
Best Time: Sunrise and early morning
Suggested Lens Length: 18-50mm

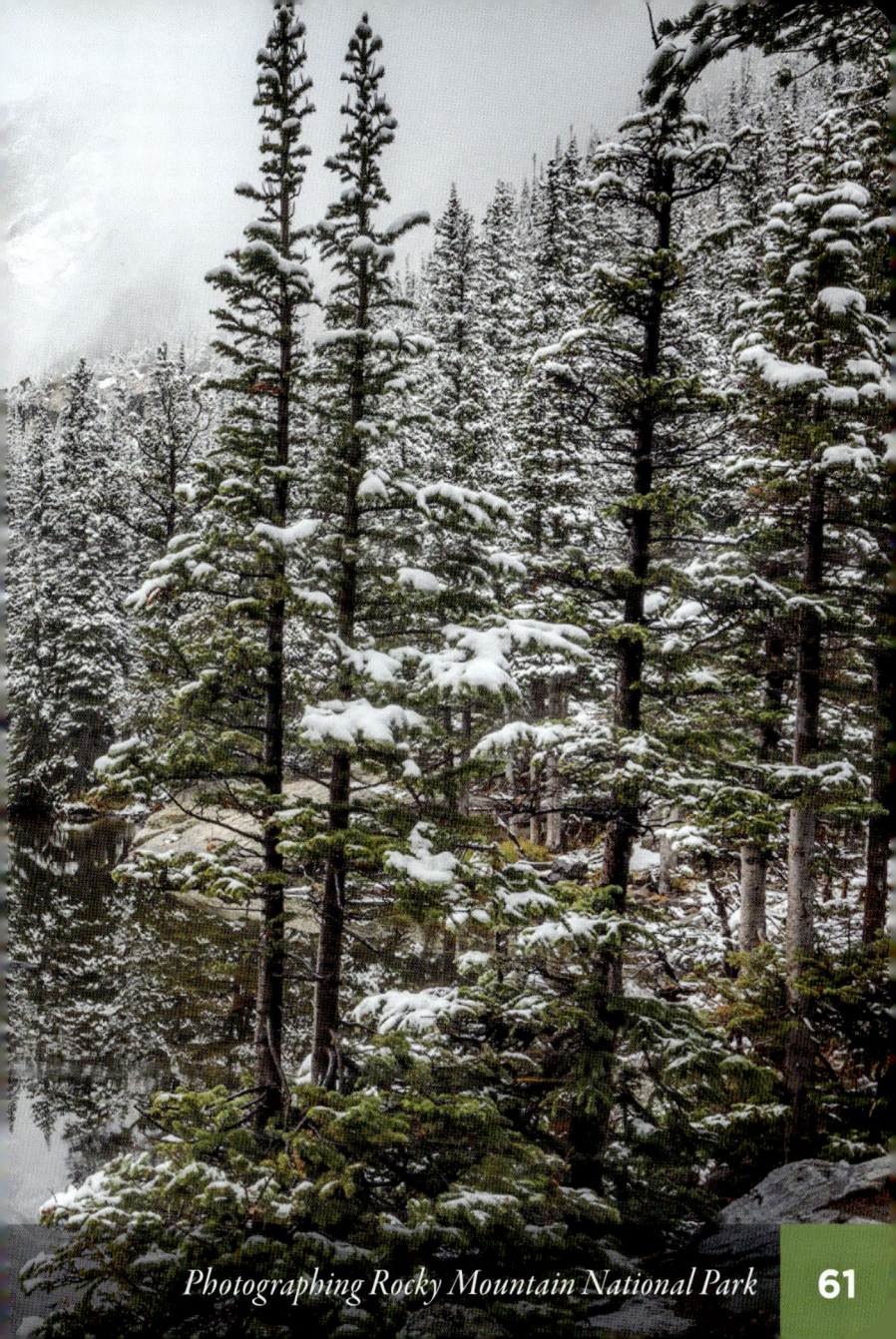

EMERALD LAKE

Just a little over half a mile past Dream Lake you will find Emerald Lake. With its green-tinted water, it lives up to its name and is an absolutely spectacular setting with granite walls climbing straight up from the lake. As with most locations on the east side of the park, the best time to photograph it is at sunrise, when the mountains can turn deep red.

Since this lake is so close to the mountains, you will need a very wide-angle lens, somewhere in the range of 14–18mm. With a wide lens you can capture some great reflection shots or include the old tree by the shoreline to help guide the viewer's eye into the photo.

In July and early August, you may also find a lot of wildflowers, especially columbines, growing along the southern shore of Emerald Lake. Columbines seem to prefer such rocky terrain. These flowers are incredibly beautiful but difficult to photograph, as they tend to sway in the slightest breeze. Watch your footsteps so you don't damage them or the soil they are growing in.

In the spring and early summer, it is not uncommon to have a small waterfall coming down the side of the slope below Hallett Peak. This can be incorporated into your images as well, and the sound of the falling water echoing

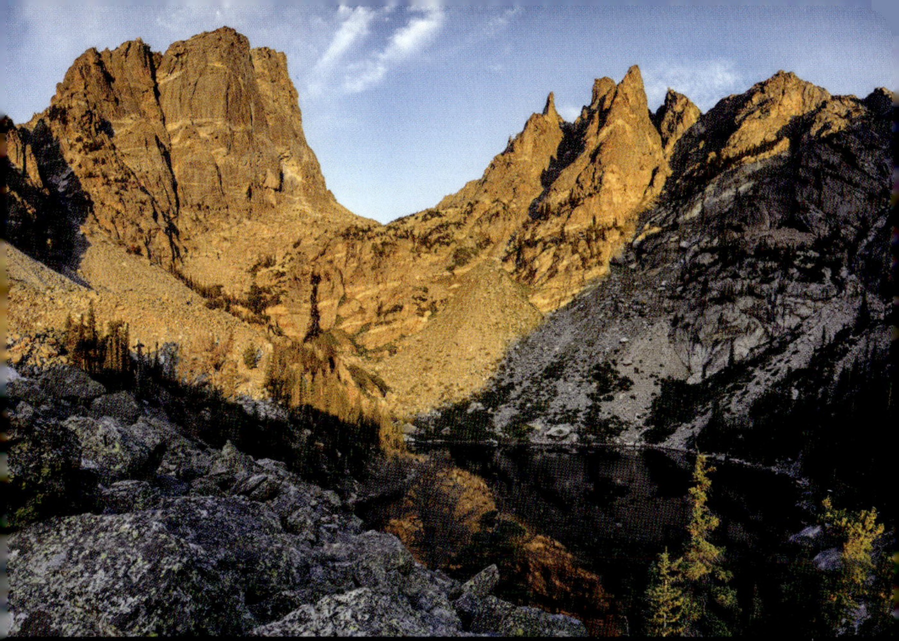

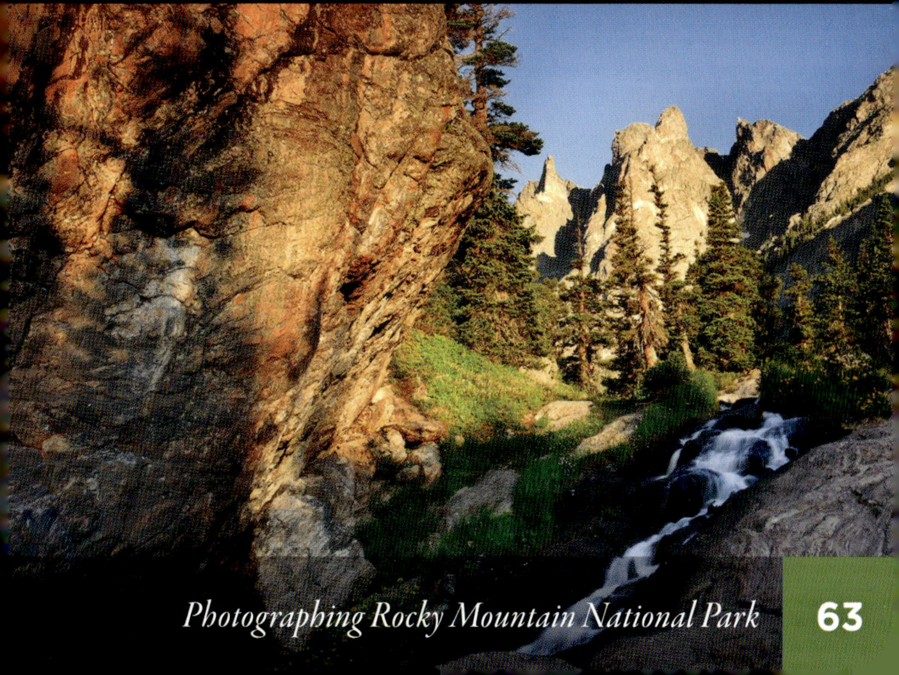

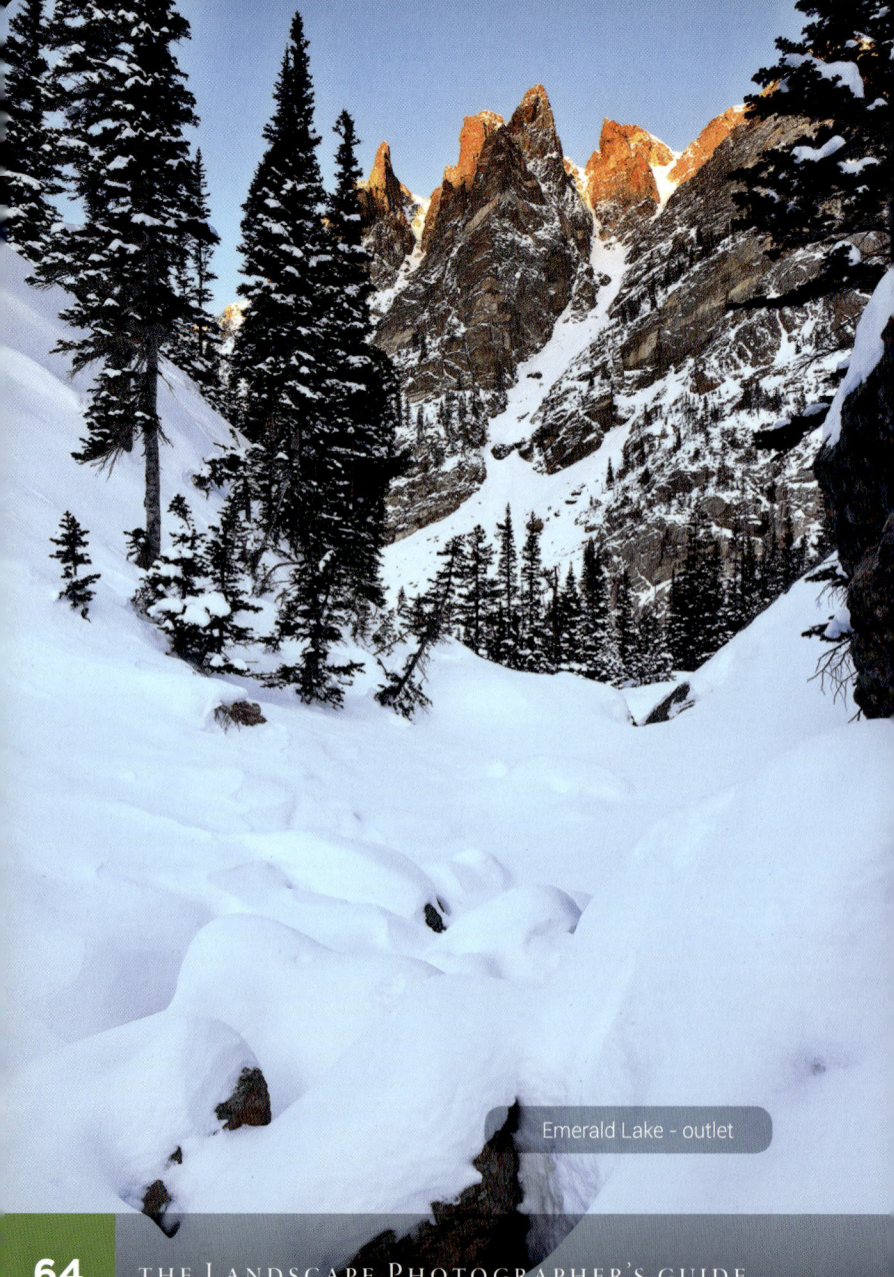

Emerald Lake - outlet

about within this amphitheater is a real delight.

If you don't have such a wide lens, there are other options. One option is to climb up the rocks on the southeast side of the lake until you are high enough to include the lake and one of the peaks in your frame of view. This gives a real sense of the ruggedness of the place.

Another option is to head back down the trail a few hundred feet from the lake and capture the tree-lined meadow with Flattop Mountain towering above it. There are a number of interesting compositions to be had from here, such as including the trail leading up toward the mountain.

Another possibility in the area is to head down to about halfway between Dream Lake and Emerald Lake to where a turn in the trail is next to a large rock slab with a large rock wall behind it. Here you can photograph the small stream running down the rock with Flattop Mountain high above it. About twenty minutes after the beginning of sunrise, the rock wall will light up as well and create a wonderfully rugged scene.

LAKE HAIYAHA

If you are looking for another option near Bear Lake but one that isn't quite as popular, Lake Haiyaha should fit the bill. The hike is a little over two miles from the Bear Lake Trailhead. First follow the trail up to Nymph and Dream lakes. Just before the trail reaches Dream Lake there is an intersection. Follow it to the left and continue up the rather steep climb to Lake Haiyaha. On the way up you will be afforded a couple of spectacular viewpoints out toward the backside of Longs Peak. These overlooks are great places from which to photograph in the evening or at sunset.

Continue along the trail until you reach the sign directing you toward Lake Haiyaha. After about a third of a mile the trail skirts a small pond surrounded by large boulders. This is not the actual lake itself but is often a better place to photograph, as the surrounding rocks protect it from wind, allowing you a better chance of capturing reflections. From here you can get a good view of Hallett Peak.

After you've shot this pond, continue along the somewhat obscure trail to the lake itself. On the way you will find a very old tree that has a lot of character and makes for unusual subject matter. As you make your way, you'll

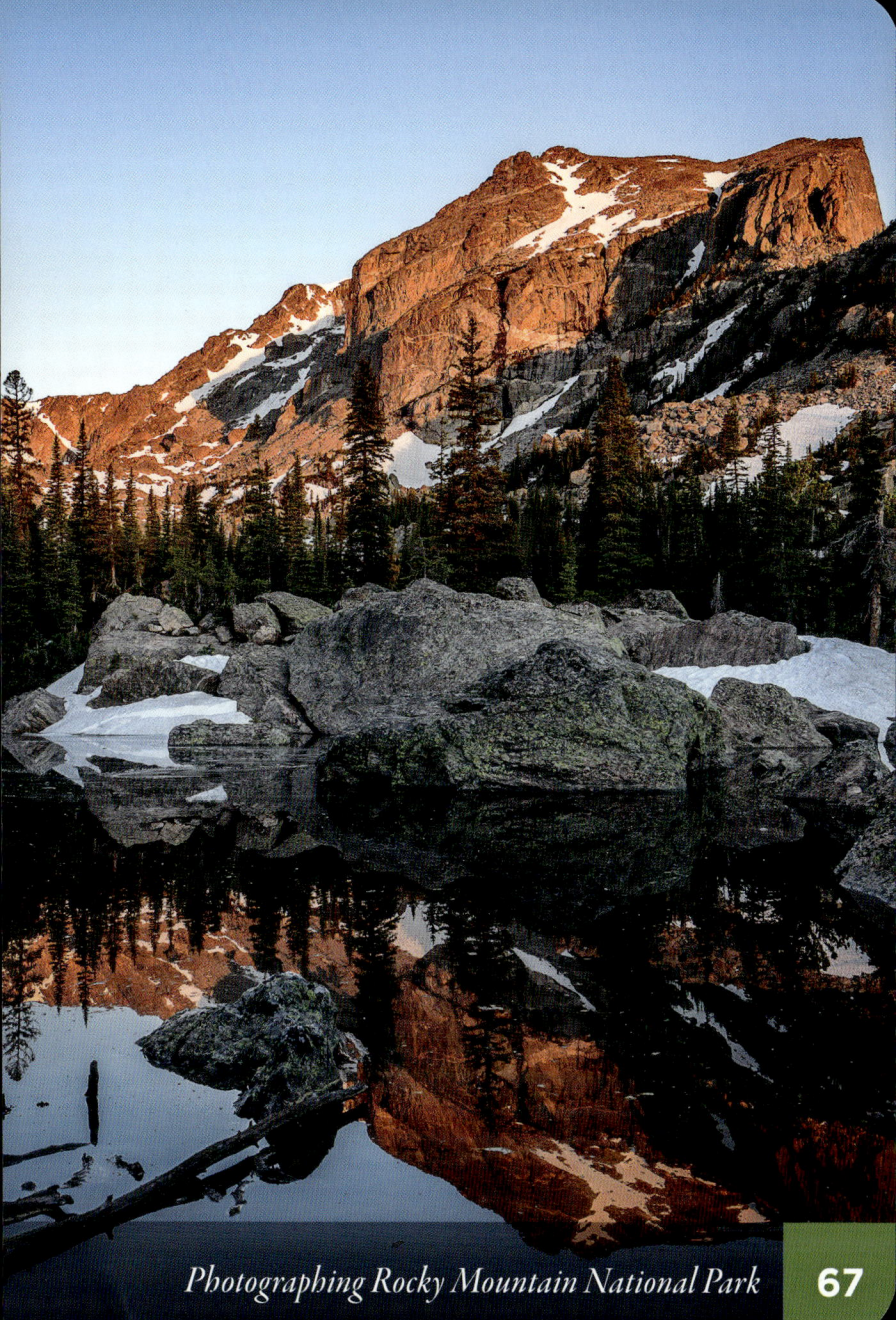

find yourself having to do a fair amount of rock hopping, since the entire valley is filled with giant boulders. Not surprisingly, the name Haiyaha is actually the Arapahoe word for "big rocks." Take extra care as you crawl across the boulders, as it would be easy to break an ankle here. Also, if the rocks are wet, they will be extremely slippery and should not be climbed.

Once you reach the lake itself you can crawl down to several rocks right along the shore of the lake to photograph. On a windless day I focus on reflections. If the wind is blowing, I might find a composition in the midst of the boulders. The compositional options in the area are endless, so feel free to experiment.

Lake Haiyaha is also spectacular during the winter, particularly at sunrise; however, you will need to take an alternate route to get there. In the winter the trail from Dream Lake to Lake Haiyaha should not be used, as it is prone to avalanches. Instead, begin at the Glacier Gorge Trailhead and follow the alternate route.

LAKE HELENE

An absolutely stunning location to photograph in the Bear Lake area is Lake Helene. It lies just to the north of Flattop Mountain at the base of Notchtop Mountain, which towers over the lake. From a distance, Notchtop doesn't look that impressive, as it blends in with the rest of the Continental Divide, but as you get close to it, the majesty of this mountain is breathtaking.

To reach Lake Helene requires a bit more energy than most of the other places mentioned so far. It is close to three and a half miles from Bear Lake, making it an almost seven-mile round trip. The trailhead for this hike

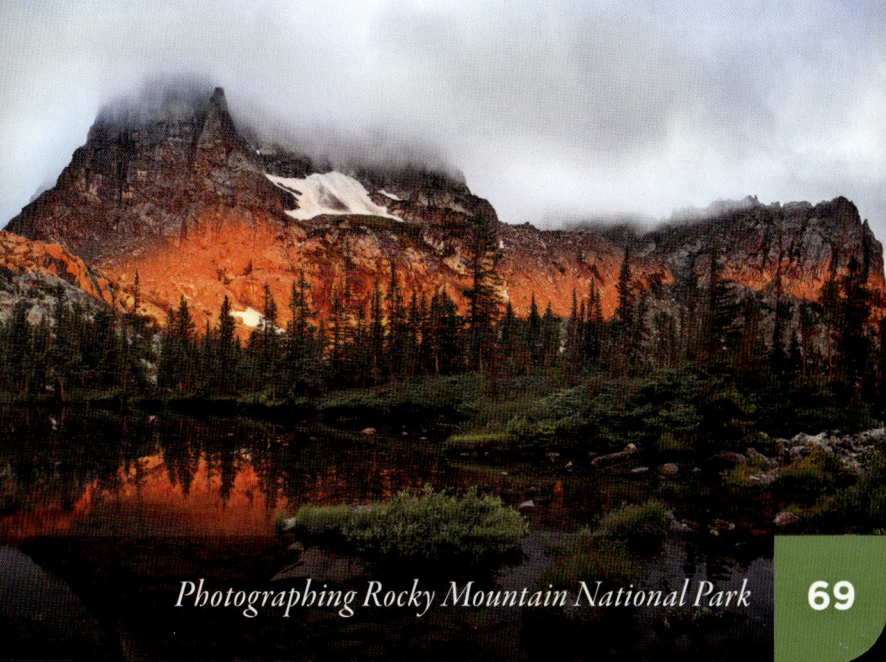

begins on the northeast side of Bear Lake and follows the Fern Lake Trail. As you finally near the base of Notchtop, the trail gently begins to head downhill. Watch for a small path heading off to your left. This will take you down to Lake Helene. If the trail begins to descend steeply in a northerly direction, you have missed the turn.

The views from Lake Helene and the surrounding area are spectacular year round. However, the trail can often be hard to find in the winter and early spring when the blowing snow hides the trail. There is also one slope that is prone to avalanches. Because of these factors, I only recommend this hike during summer and early fall.

At the lake itself, you will find the best compositions to be had near the outlet stream. When the water level is low, you may be able to boulder-hop a little to the east and find a few more options. In order to shoot this scene, you will definitely need a very wide-angle lens.

After you have shot Notchtop over Lake Helene, head back to the main trail and continue downward for a short distance. You will be rewarded with wonderful views of Grace Falls, which pours off the base of the mountain on its way down to Lake Odessa.

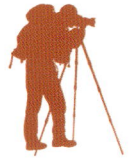

HIGHWAY 7

When most people visit Rocky Mountain National Park, they often forget about Highway 7, as this road is not actually inside the park but follows the eastern edge of Rocky and provides many spectacular views and photo opportunities.

LILY LAKE

Located directly off of Highway 7, about six miles south of Estes Park, Lily Lake is another easily accessible jewel of Rocky Mountain National Park. This alpine lake is a favorite for anglers, casual walkers, and families; it's also a great place for photography.

Lily Lake is one of the newest additions to Rocky Mountain National Park, having been acquired by park partners in 1992. It sits just below Twin Sisters Peaks and affords beautiful views of Longs Peak to the south and the Mummy Range to the northwest. A gentle accessible trail runs around the lake.

This is a great sunrise location. When you get to the lake turn right and continue until you reach the bridge that lies on the northeast corner. From here you have a great perspective of Longs Peak, Mount Meeker, and Estes Cone high above the lake. In the morning these often light up dramatically.

There are also several great spots above the lake. Just before the bridge on the northeast corner is a small trail that heads off to the right. Follow this and it will lead you along the north end of the lake but with a completely different point of view than you'll get from the path below. From up here you can see the entire lake with Longs Peak behind it. There are some benches nestled here for you to take the time to drink in the view.

If you continue around to the northwest corner of the lake you'll find a small trail leading away from the lake. Follow this trail to get a view of the Mummy Range. You may have to climb up on some rocks to get an unobstructed view.

Along the southern shore there is also a lot to capture.

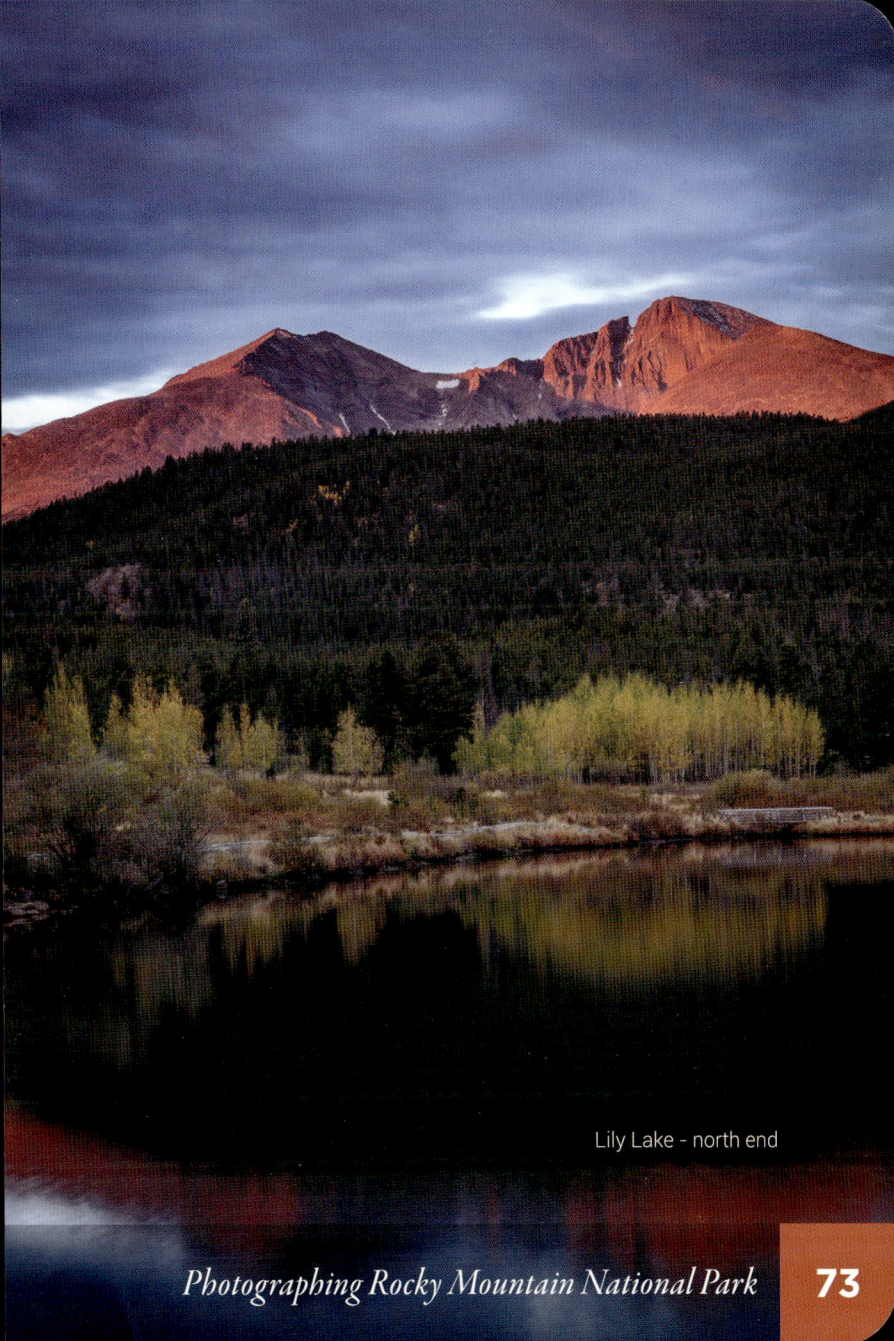

Lily Lake - north end

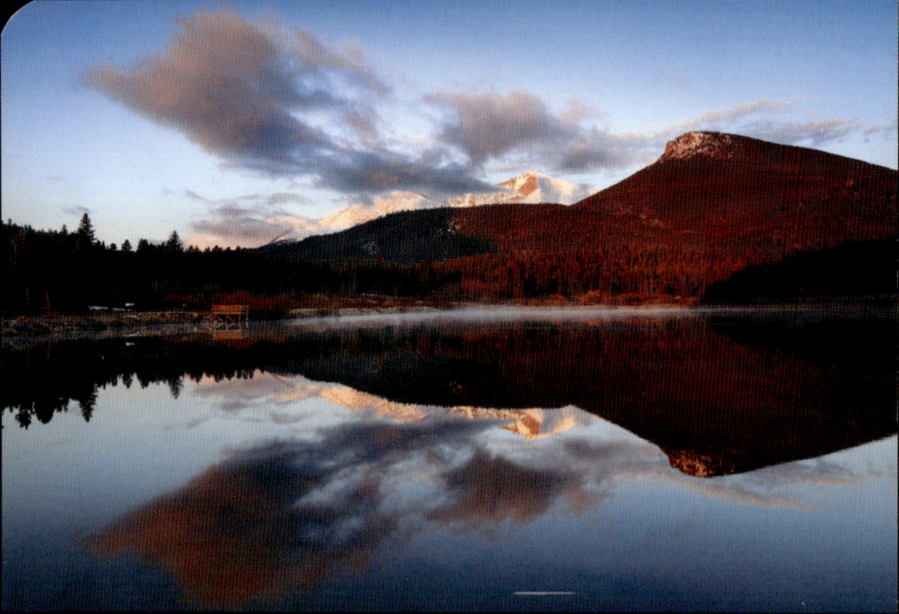

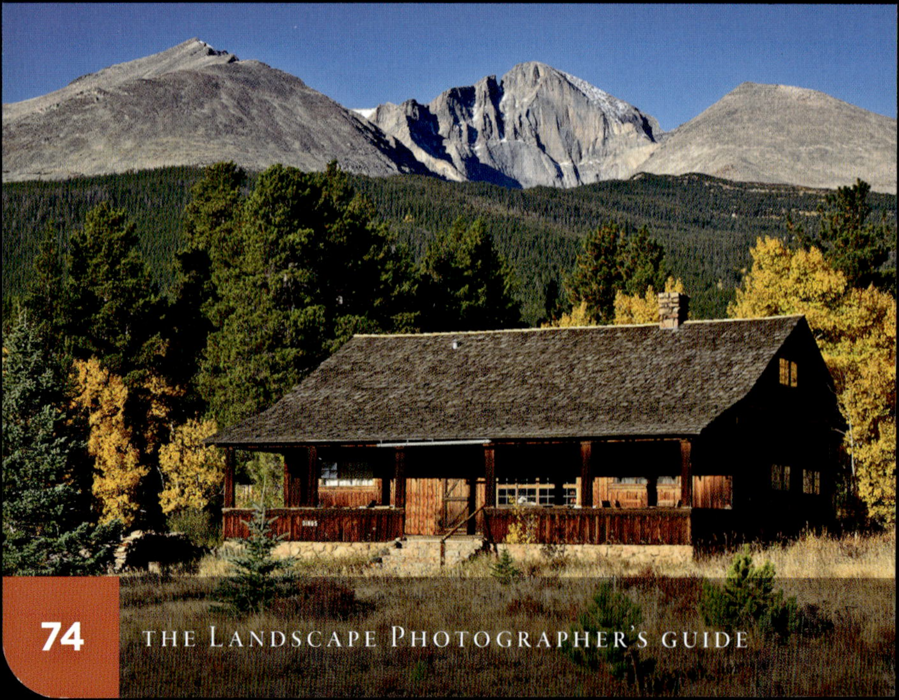

You can photograph looking to the north to highlight the unusual rocks that tower above the lake. On this side of the lake you will find a marshy area that is frequented by a large variety of birds during the late spring and early summer. Also on the south end of the lake is a grove of aspen trees, which take on vibrant colors in the spring and autumn. These aspens can be included in shots of Longs Peak. Finally, along the southern end of the lake you'll find one of the best places to find pasqueflowers growing under the ponderosa trees during the early spring.

LONGS PEAK VIEW

High above all other mountains in Rocky Mountain National Park stands Longs Peak. At 14,259 feet, Longs Peak with its distinctive shape can be seen across the Front Range from way south in Colorado Springs all the way into Wyoming. It calls attention to itself with its icy crown that touches the sky.

Every angle of Longs Peak is quite unique, and people often don't realize that they are seeing the same mountain when viewing it from another side. Without a doubt, the most recognized view of Longs Peak is from the east. The sheer east face known as "the Diamond" and "the Notch" next to it are widely recognized.

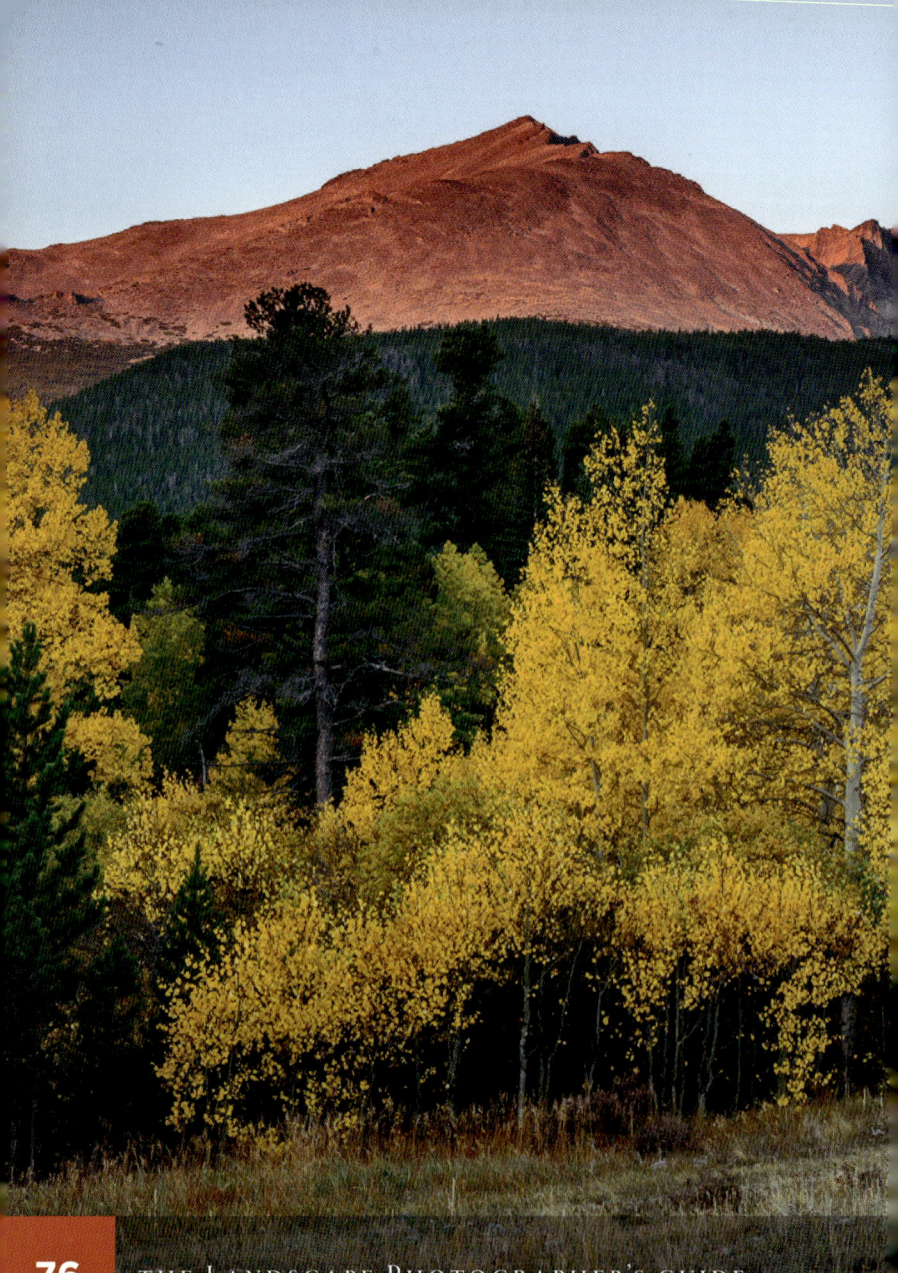

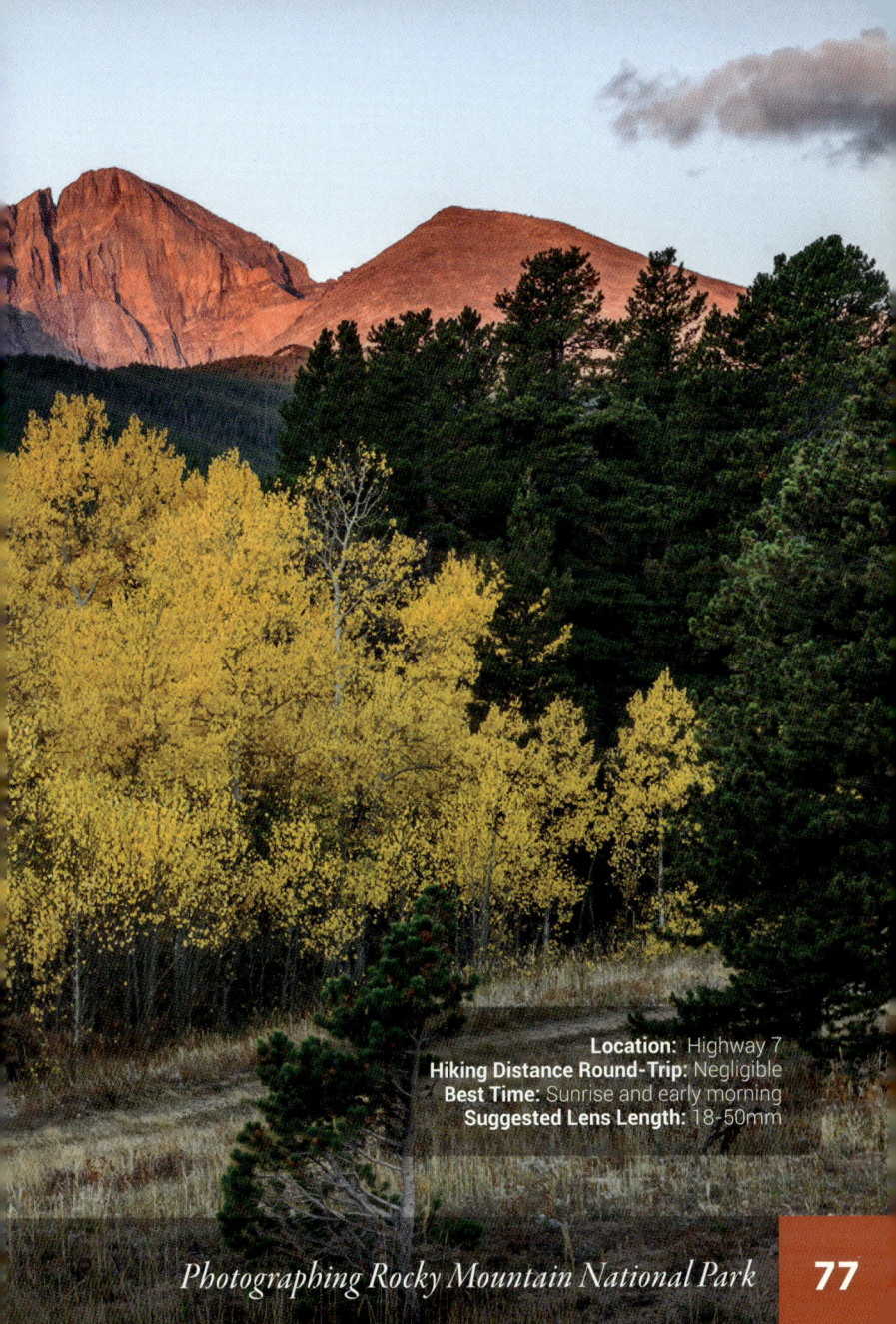

Location: Highway 7
Hiking Distance Round-Trip: Negligible
Best Time: Sunrise and early morning
Suggested Lens Length: 18-50mm

Probably the best location from which to photograph the eastern face of Longs Peak is Highway 7 between Estes Park and Allenspark. Along this road there are numerous views of the massive peak. The best stretch from which to shoot begins just opposite Aspen Lodge and continues south until you reach the entrance to High Peak Camp. There are many options along the road where you can capture Longs Peak, Mount Meeker, and Mount Lady Washington looking down on the meadow. Do not cross the fence, as the meadow is private property.

Just south of the entrance to High Peak Camp is a small wooden cabin that's extremely photogenic. It is framed by aspen trees, and Longs Peak stands right behind it. Remember that this is private property, so stay on the road or shoot from the opposite side of the road.

If you're willing to hike, there is also a great overlook with views of Longs Peak along the trail leading up to Twin Sisters Peaks. The trail begins just across the road from Lily Lake. The overlook is up the trail about two miles. Don't stop at the first place where you can see Longs through the trees, but continue until you have a nice open view. I like to be up here about thirty minutes before sunrise to get the occasional predawn glow.

CHASM LAKE

This is a longer and more difficult hike but must be included in this booklet, as it is one of the most magnificent places in Rocky Mountain National Park. Chasm Lake sits on the east side of Longs Peak at an elevation of nearly 12,000 feet. Towering granite walls, some rising 2,000 feet above the lake, surround it on three sides. When the morning light hits this amphitheater, the entire area glows with the most magical light.

The hike to Chasm Lake is a little over four miles each way with an elevation gain of just over 2,000 feet. The trail begins at the Longs Peak Trailhead off of Highway 7. From the start, the trail takes a fairly steep ascent, passing several cascades and waterfalls on its way to tree line. The trees then give way to spectacular views of Colorado's Front Range to the east, while to the west Longs Peak looms overhead.

Along the way, there are two locations from which I love to shoot, as well as many other possibilities. The first one is from the junction of the Chasm Meadow spur and the Longs Peak Trail. You will know you're there when you see the triangle horse tie-up. The views from here to Longs Peak and Mount Meeker are breathtaking.

Continue along the trail toward Chasm Lake and you

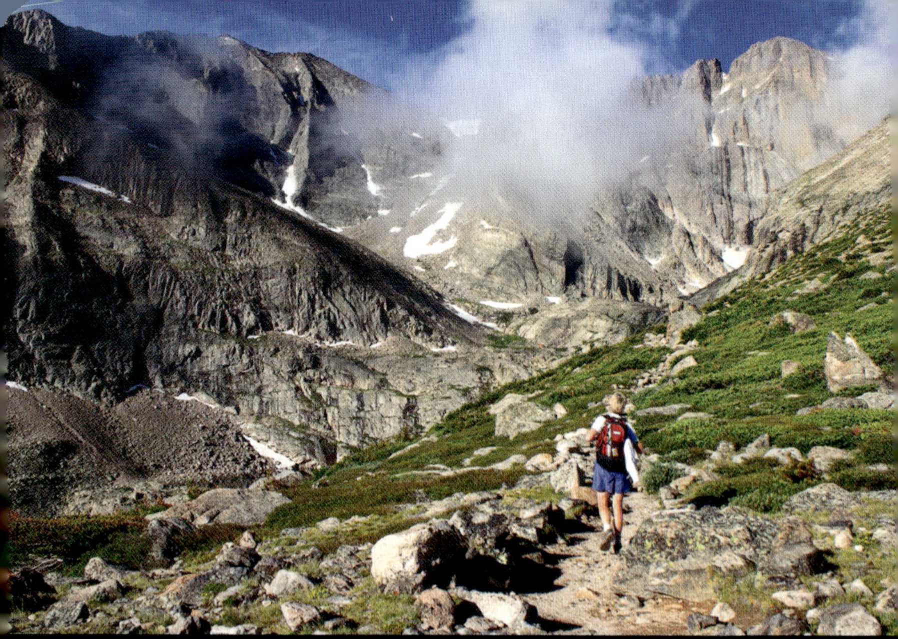

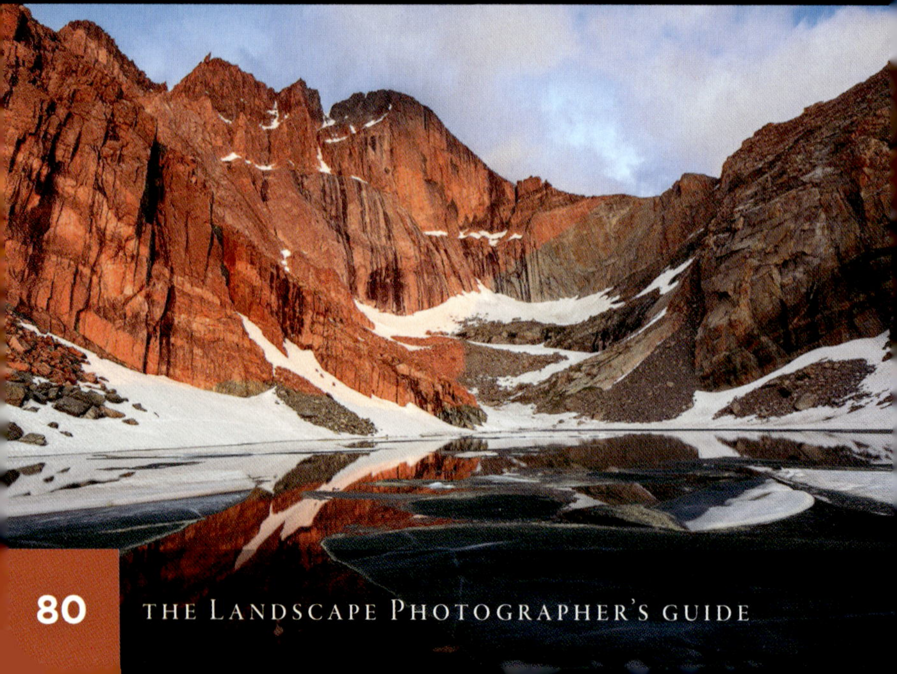

will reach the lush area of Chasm Meadow, complete with streams and a couple of waterfalls. This is one of my favorite areas. There are so many different compositional options to be found here. You can get nice reflection shots of Longs Peak in the tarns or stream. Alternatively, show the trail leading up to the peaks or zoom in on one of the waterfalls.

It is a bit of a scramble to get up to Chasm Lake, so if you're not surefooted you may find it better to shoot at one of the other locations. If you do make the scramble, you'll discover one of the most breathtaking amphitheaters you have probably ever seen. Once you are up there, you'll find numerous options. If you have a very wide-angle lens, you can get close to the lake to take advantage of reflections. If you don't have a wide enough lens for this, find a vantage point higher up the hill away from the lake. If at all possible, try to be here just as the sun rises.

Be aware that accessing this area before the snow has fully melted can be dangerous, as there is one section between Chasm Junction and Chasm Meadow that can be treacherous. If you encounter snow along this stretch, do not cross it unless you have proper training and equipment; there have been numerous incidents here.

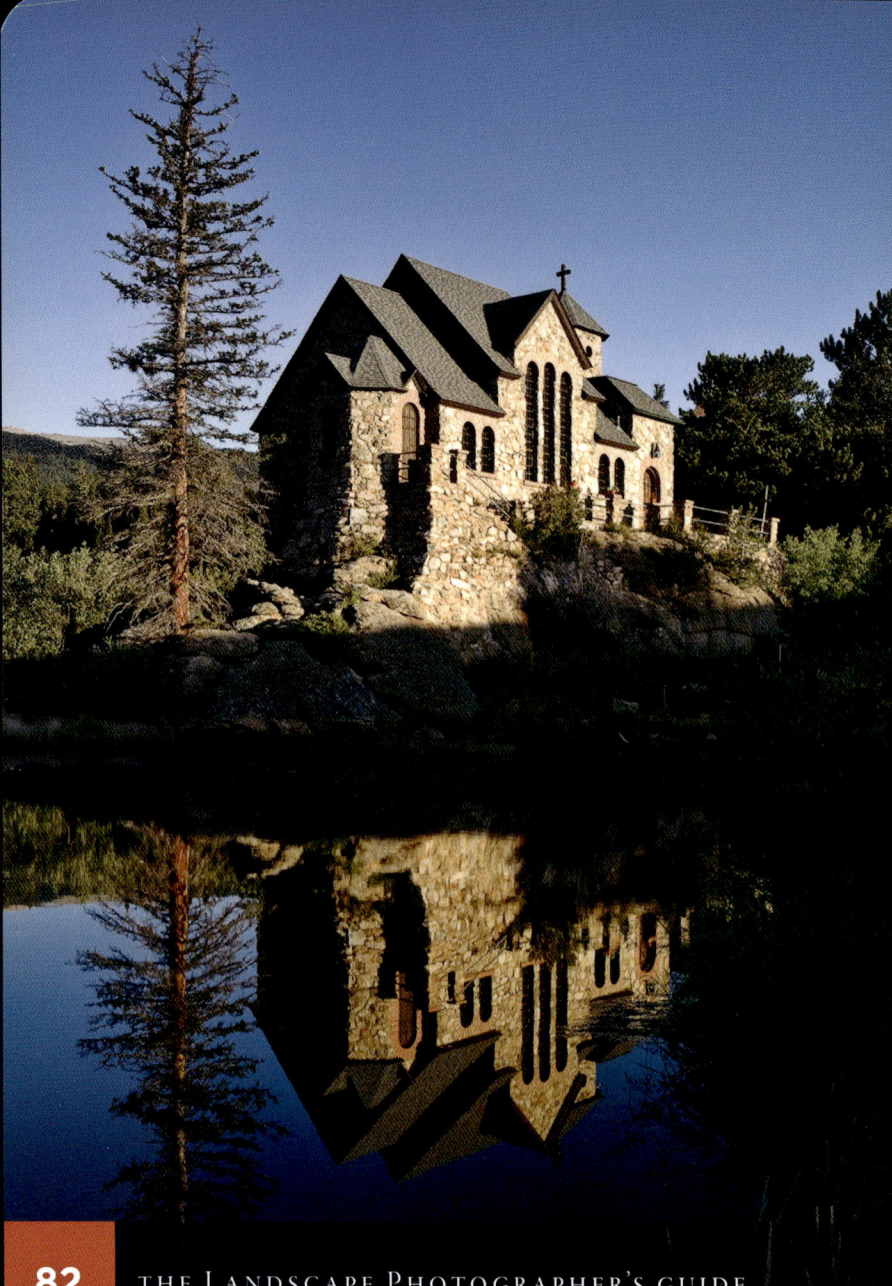

SAINT CATHERINE

Along Highway 7 near mile marker 11 the trees along the road open up, revealing a beautiful little church built upon a rock with Mount Meeker as a backdrop. This viewpoint simply begs to be photographed. The Catholic church is called Saint Catherine and is on the property of what was previously the Saint Malo Retreat Center. A fire in 2012 followed by a flood in 2013 destroyed much of the retreat center, but the church survived.

The best views of the church can be had right from the highway. This is a spot that can be photographed all year long. It is generally best photographed from sunrise through midmorning. At sunrise Mount Meeker will often glow. If you want light on the church itself, that often takes another forty-five minutes to an hour.

Occasionally the church is open for weddings or visits by the public. If you get a chance to go inside, take the opportunity. There is also a small visitor center just west of the church that's well worth a visit. They should be able to tell you when it might be open.

ALLENSPARK AREA

Allenspark is a quirky little mountain town on the south-east corner of RMNP along Highway 7. It has about 600 residents who live there year round, a fun little eatery called Meadow Mountain Cafe, which is great for lunch, and an amazing five-star restaurant called the Fawn Brook Inn. The town also has a little log church that is very photogenic both inside and out.

My favorite locations to shoot around Allenspark can be found just north of the fire station and waste transfer station on Highway 7. There is a large pull-over space here where you can park and enjoy the view. From here you can capture Mount Meeker above a stand of aspen trees. In the spring they are brilliant green and in the autumn they are gorgeous yellow.

Another good place to photograph in the Allenspark area can be found about two miles north of town on Highway 7, just a little south of the turn for Wild Basin, where the highway crosses the North Saint Vrain Creek. From the bridge you can capture fabulous views of the Wild Basin area with its lofty peaks. I particularly like to come here when there is fresh snow and the willows are bright orange in early spring, but it works well all year round. You may have to work a little to avoid the power

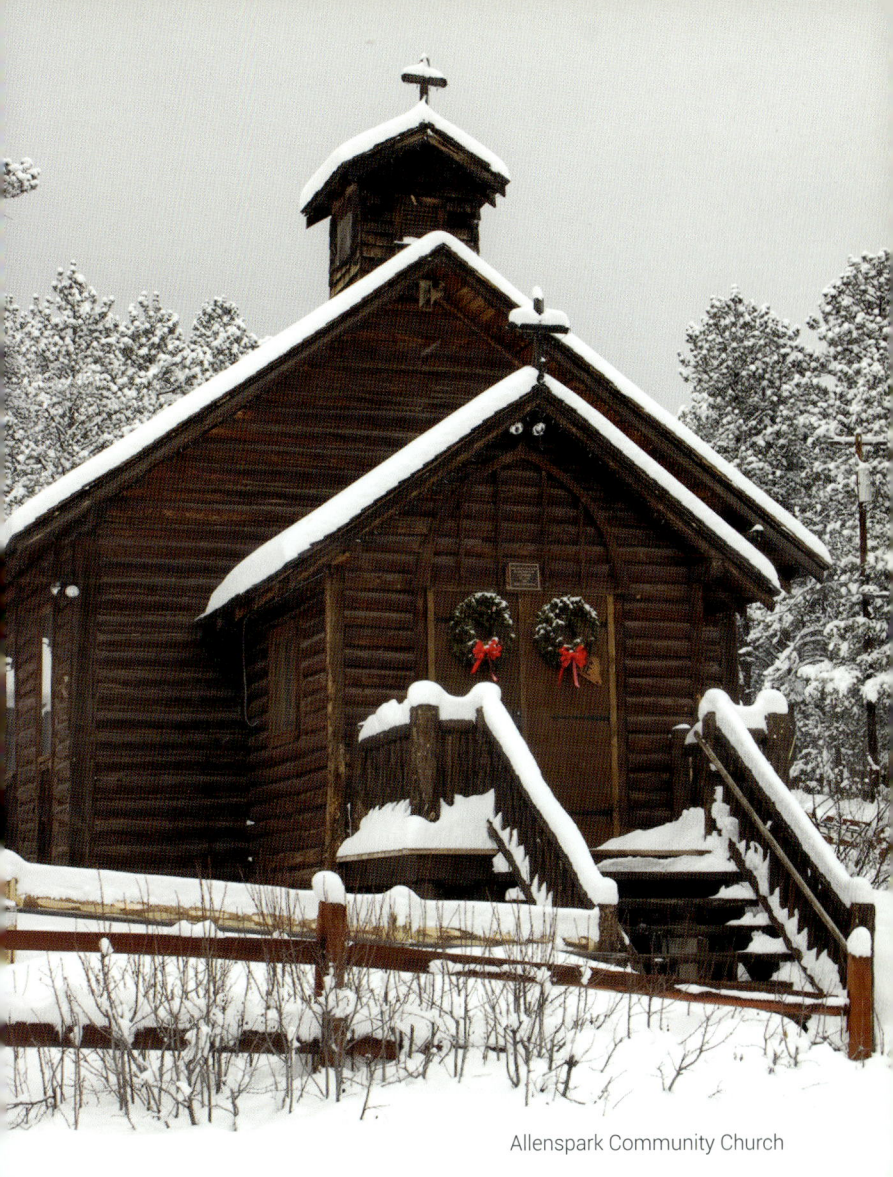

Allenspark Community Church

lines that were put in a rather unfortunate location, as far as photography goes. I've spoken with the power company but have not yet been able to convince them to move the lines. I'll keep trying.

WILD BASIN

Wild Basin is one of the lesser-known areas of Rocky Mountain National Park. It contains some of the most stunning lakes and scenery, but most of the best locations are 6–8 miles from the trailhead. I will not cover these more remote areas but will focus on a few places in Wild Basin that are much more accessible.

The first and easiest spot to photograph in Wild Basin is from the edge of Copeland Lake. This small lake is found just a couple of hundred feet after the entrance station. There is plenty of room to park and walk down to the water's edge. From here, there is a terrific view of the round-topped yet imposing Mount Copeland and, if the wind isn't blowing, you can capture its reflection in the still water.

If you like waterfalls or a quiet walk by a forested river, then a walk up the trail at Wild Basin is well worth your time. Begin by driving down the dirt road at Wild Basin until you reach the parking lot at its end. From here a

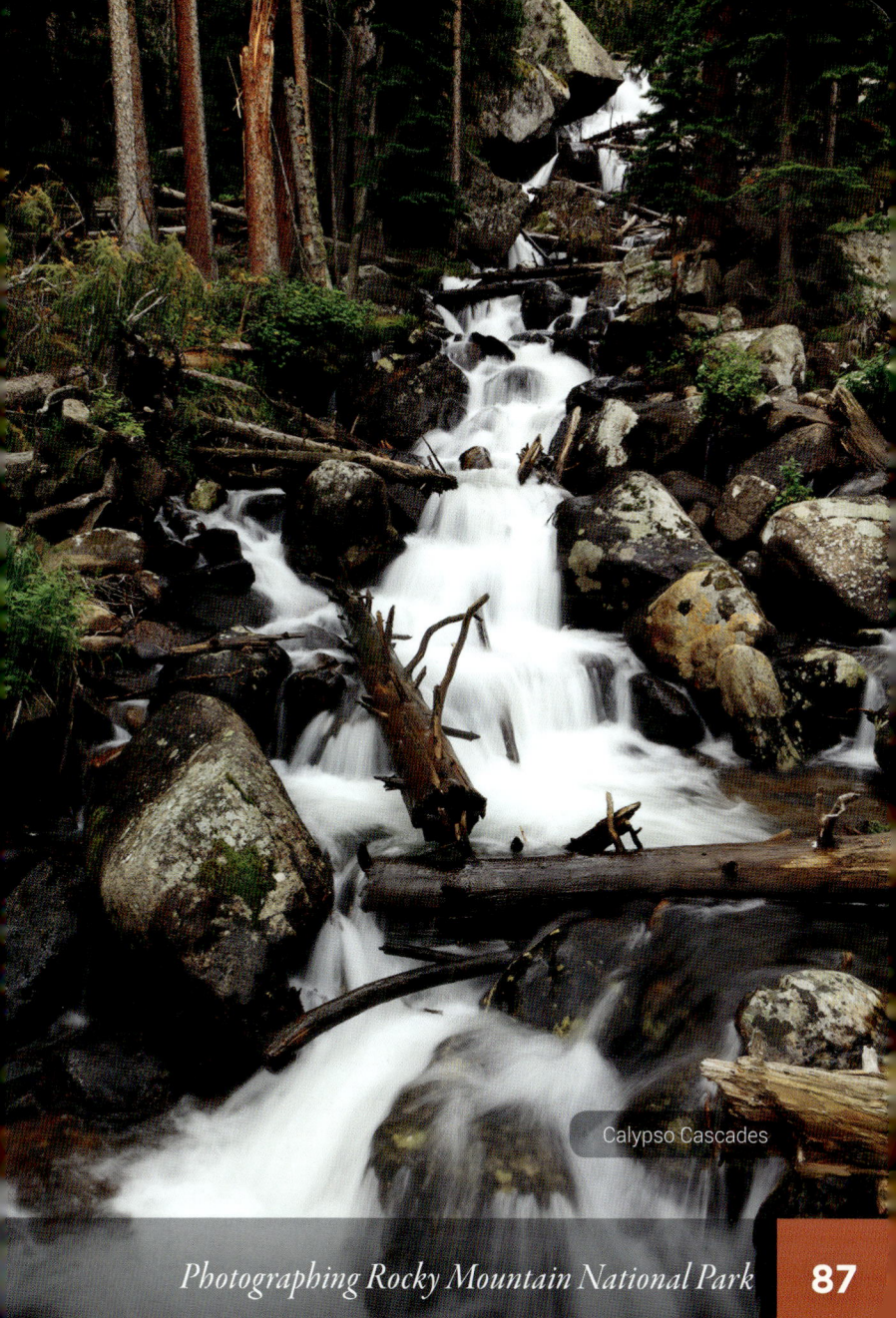

Calypso Cascades

mostly gentle trail follows the North Saint Vrain Creek for approximately two miles to Calypso Cascades. Here the water dances from rock to rock as it tumbles down several hundred feet. The roar can be almost deafening. Like most waterfalls and cascades, it is best photographed on overcast days.

If you still have energy, continue on this trail for an additional mile until you reach Ouzel Falls. There are many great compositions to be had from here, both near the bridge and up close to the waterfall. Just watch your step, as the area near the waterfall is usually quite slippery. It would be very easy to get hurt on the wet logs and rocks.

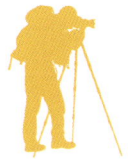

TRAIL RIDGE ROAD

There are a few roads in the United States that absolutely should not be missed, and Trail Ridge Road may be at the top of that list. It is one of America's highest paved roads, and it leads through jaw-dropping scenery with large portions of it traveling through spectacular alpine tundra. The higher portions of this road are typically closed from mid-October through late May due to the extreme alpine environment with heavy snows and high winds for much of the year.

BEAVER MEADOWS

You don't always have to drive or hike very far to enjoy beautiful views. Beaver Meadows is the area around the main entrance station on the east side of Rocky Mountain

National Park and it affords wonderful views of the high peaks as well as gentle meadows where you can often see elk, deer, and coyote.

The first scenic spot is located immediately before the main entrance station. The meadow area on the south side of the road has a great view of Longs Peak. During May and June there are often wildflowers in this meadow and elk can often be seen grazing here as well. This is a particularly terrific place to photograph from sunrise through midmorning. Try to stay on the road so as to not trample the vegetation.

Continue through the entrance station and, just after the road takes its first sharp turn to the right, watch for the small dirt road that heads to the left. Follow this dirt road to the end. As you drive along, you'll see many terrific photo opportunities you can come back and explore later. At the end of the road, park your vehicle and walk to the trailhead on the south side of the parking lot. Here you will find a stand of aspen trees that seems almost to be made for framing Longs Peak. You can also walk across the little bridge and take a photo using the trail leading through the meadow to guide the viewer's eye up to Longs Peak.

If you are up for a little hiking, walk back down the

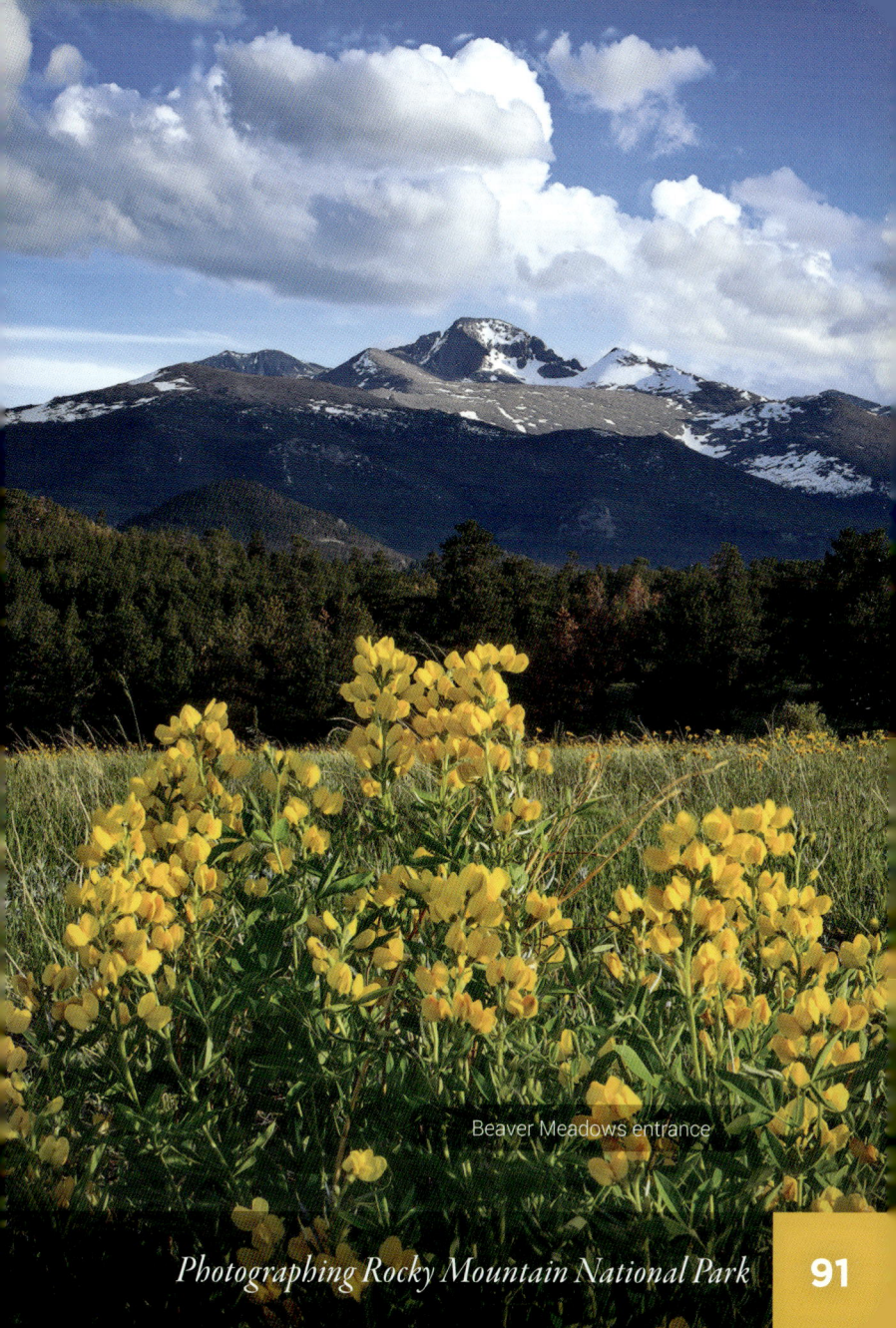

Beaver Meadows entrance

Photographing Rocky Mountain National Park

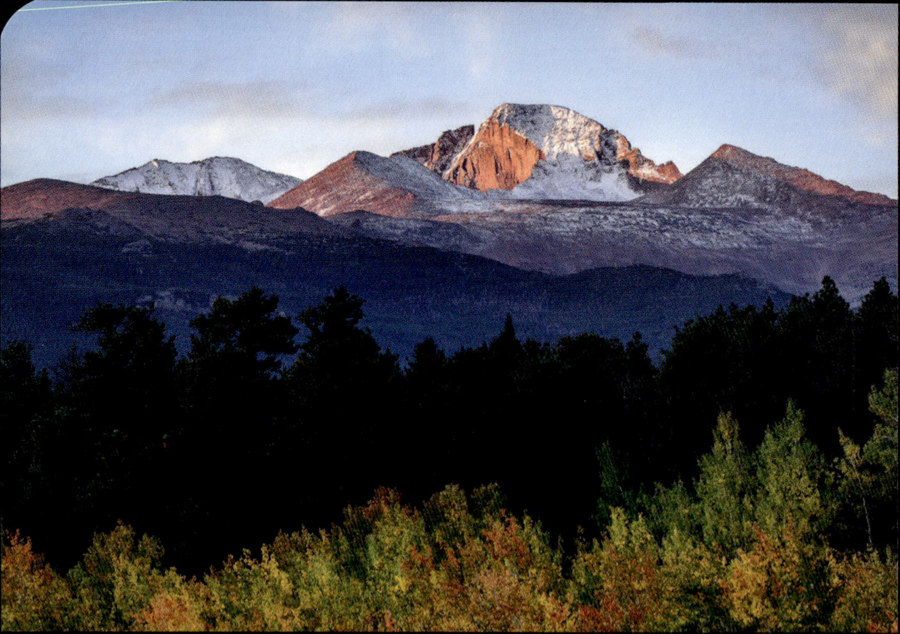

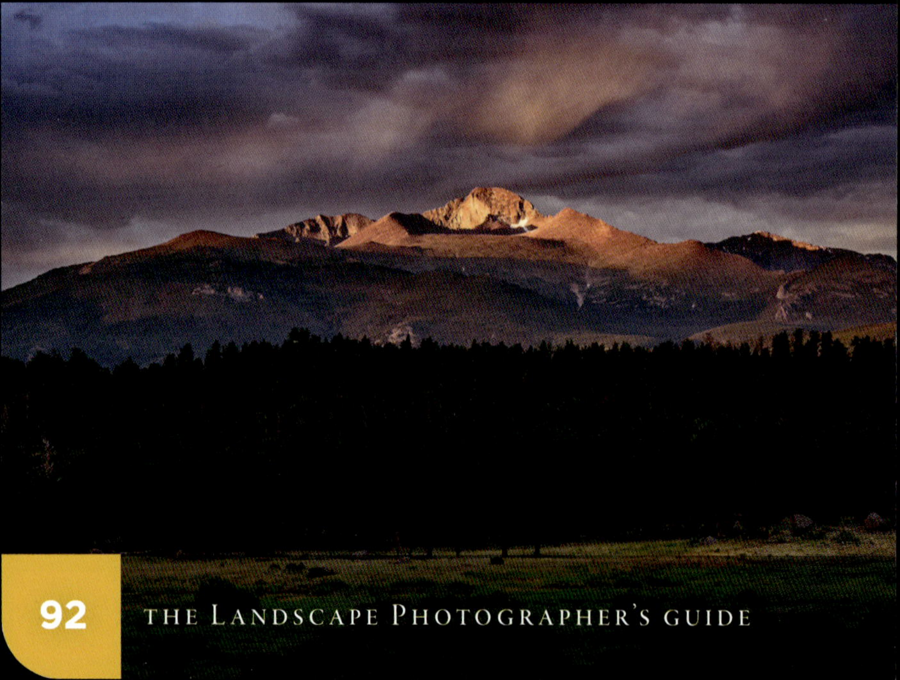

THE LANDSCAPE PHOTOGRAPHER'S GUIDE

road from the parking area until you find the trail leading off to the north. Follow this for about a mile until you are up in the meadows. This area provides dozens of great places from which to capture Longs Peak looming over the meadow. To help create that effect, use a long lens between 100–300mm to zoom in and make Longs appear very close. In the summer you can often find many flowers to help fill the foreground.

LOWER TRAIL RIDGE ROAD

If you want a quick place to go for sunrise, the lower portion of Trail Ridge Road is a very easy option, providing wide-open views of meadows and forests with jagged snow-capped mountains above them. One of the more popular locations from which to photograph along lower Trail Ridge Road is the large pull-over on the south side of Trail Ridge Road, about two and a half miles up from the entrance station. You'll know you have the right pull-over, as it is several times larger than the others and has a large information sign about the area. From here you can shoot across toward Longs Peak at sunrise and include some of the trees below you as part of the foreground of the image. Alternatively, you can put on a long lens and focus on individual peaks. There are also a number of unusual

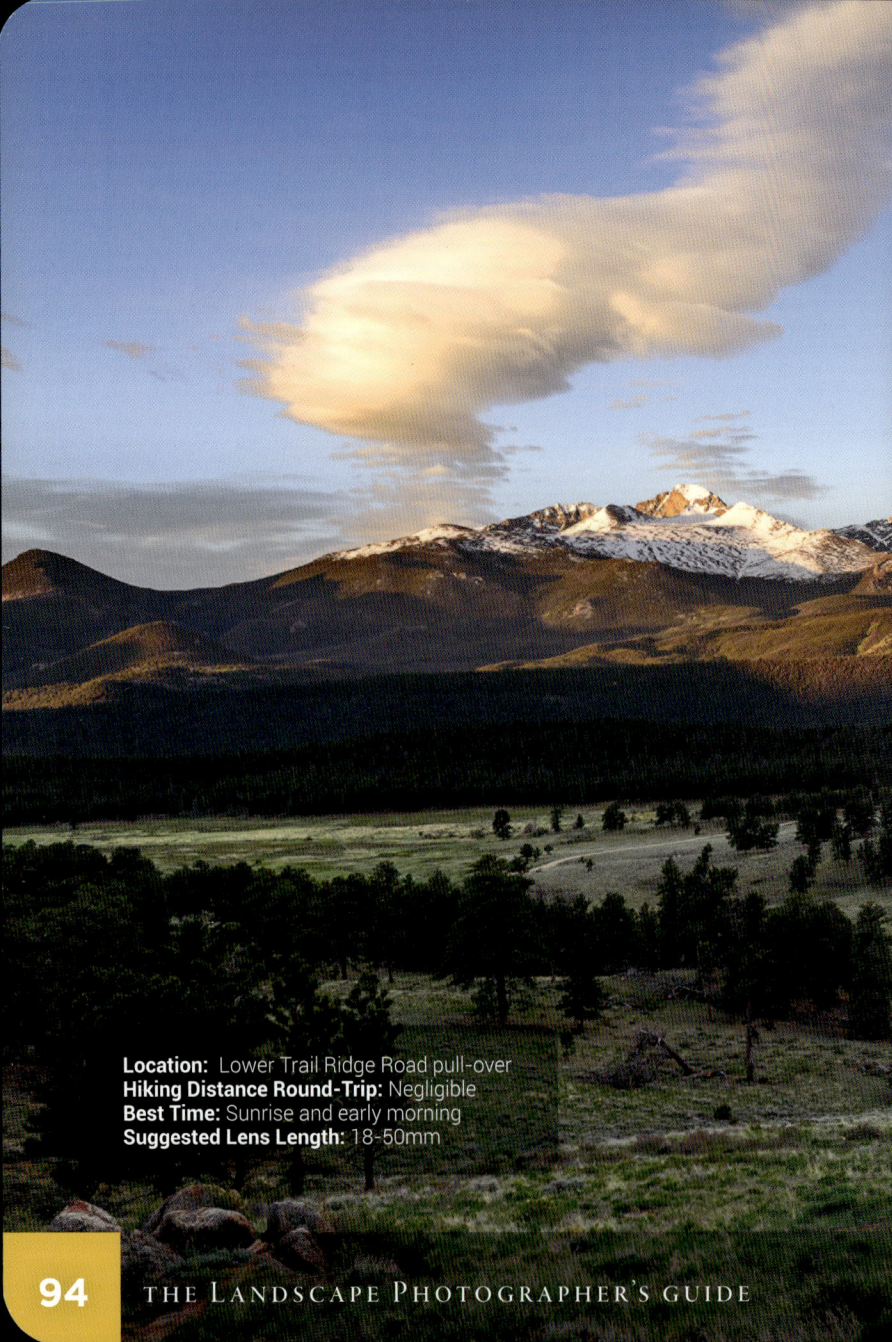

Location: Lower Trail Ridge Road pull-over
Hiking Distance Round-Trip: Negligible
Best Time: Sunrise and early morning
Suggested Lens Length: 18-50mm

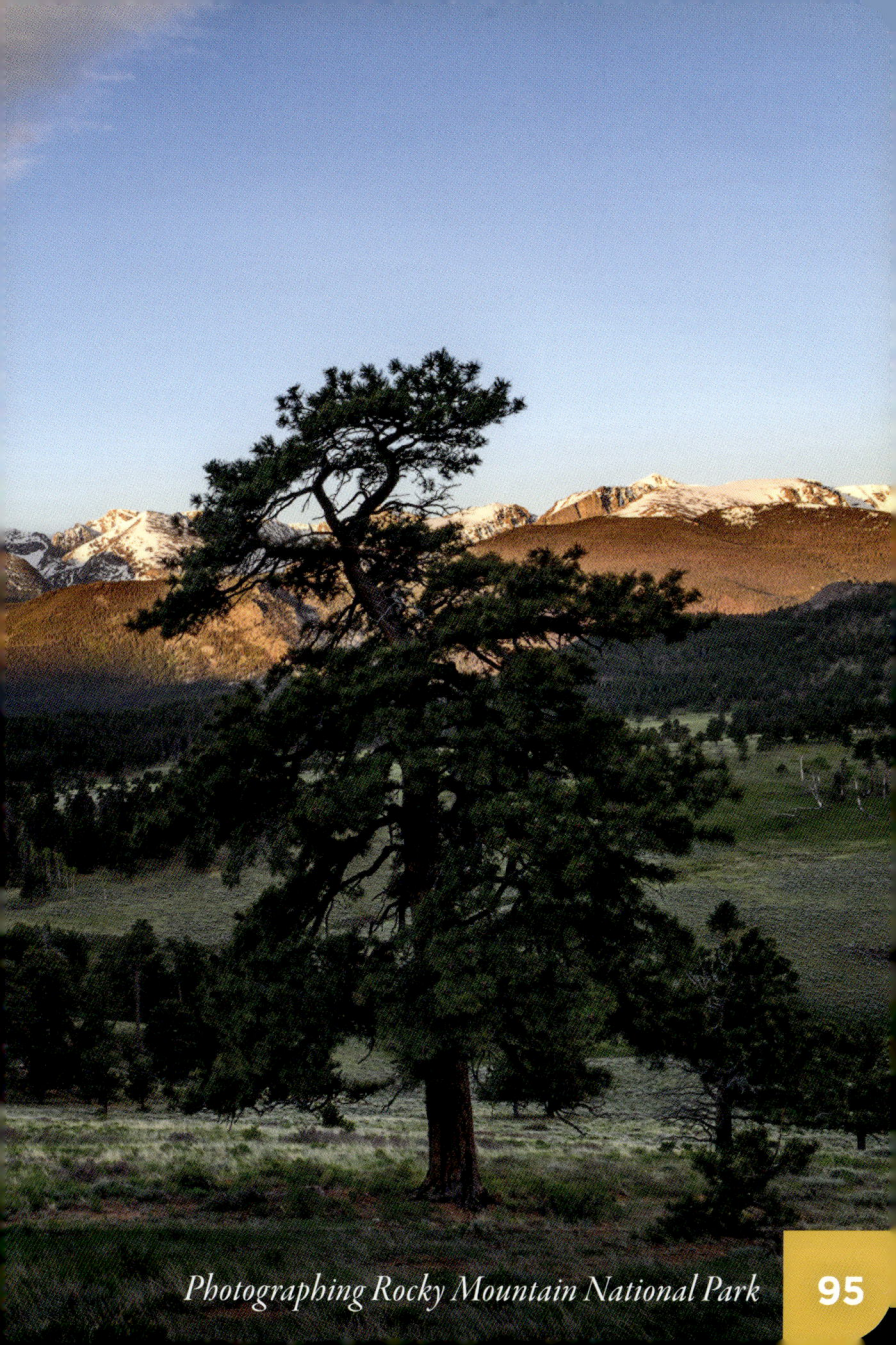

trees growing out of the rocks in this area. These make for an interesting subject on their own or in combination with the larger scene.

There are several other pull-overs along the lower portion of Trail Ridge Road where you can stop and get slightly different perspectives on the dramatic view. These are good to know about in case the main area is already busy.

Another option you have is to park at the Deer Mountain Trailhead. If you hike up the trail just over a mile you will have an even higher perspective of this same scene but will also have the advantage of having gorgeous aspen trees that you can include in your photo. Simply hike up the trail until you reach the switchbacks beside a number of lone aspen trees.

MANY PARKS CURVE & RAINBOW CURVE

On the drive up Trail Ridge Road, there are two very prominent viewpoints where everyone stops and gets out to enjoy the vistas they provide. While these are not the most photogenic locations, it is still possible to get some decent photos from these areas. The main problem is the lack of foreground material to create a sense of place to

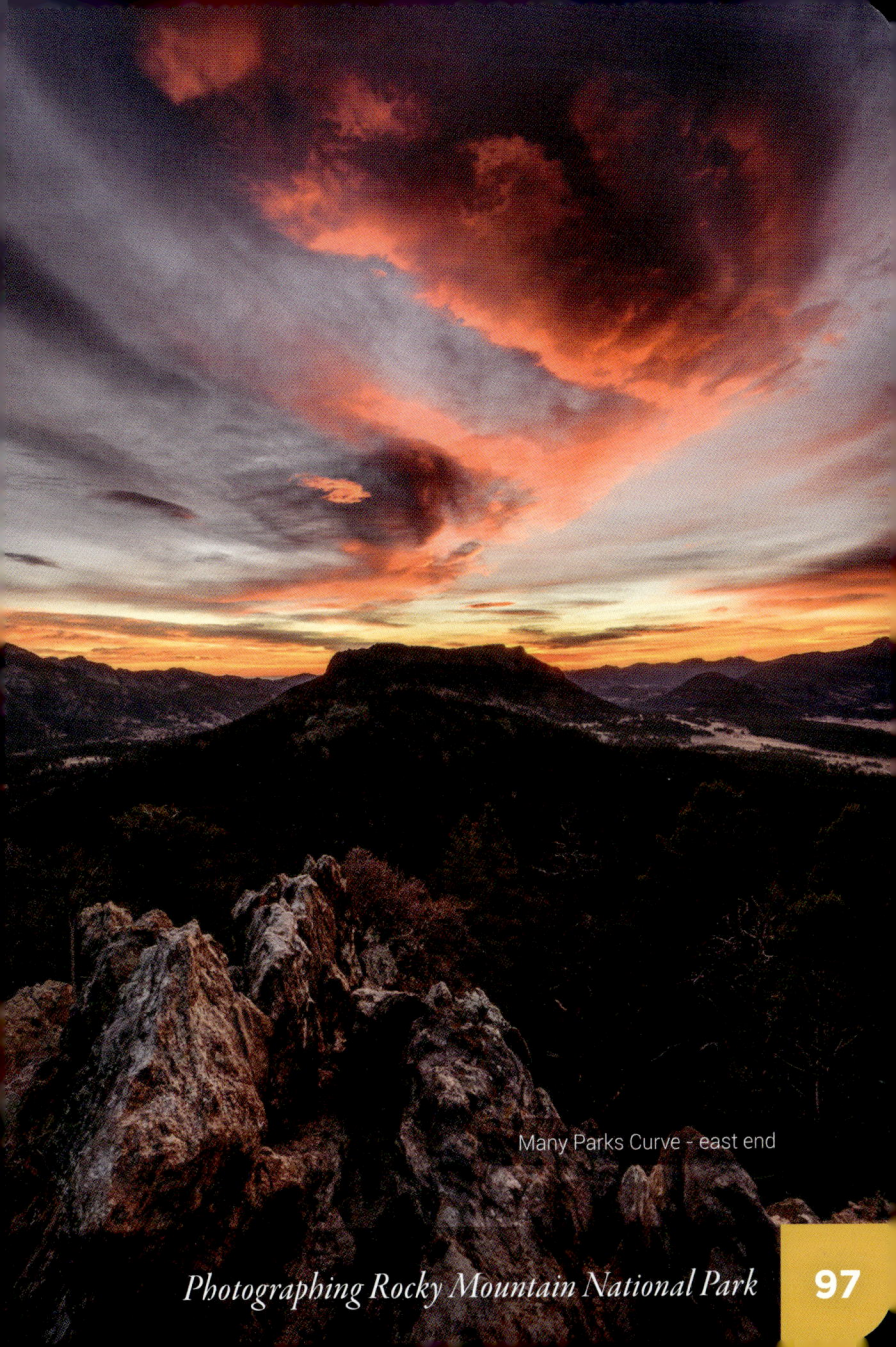

Many Parks Curve - east end

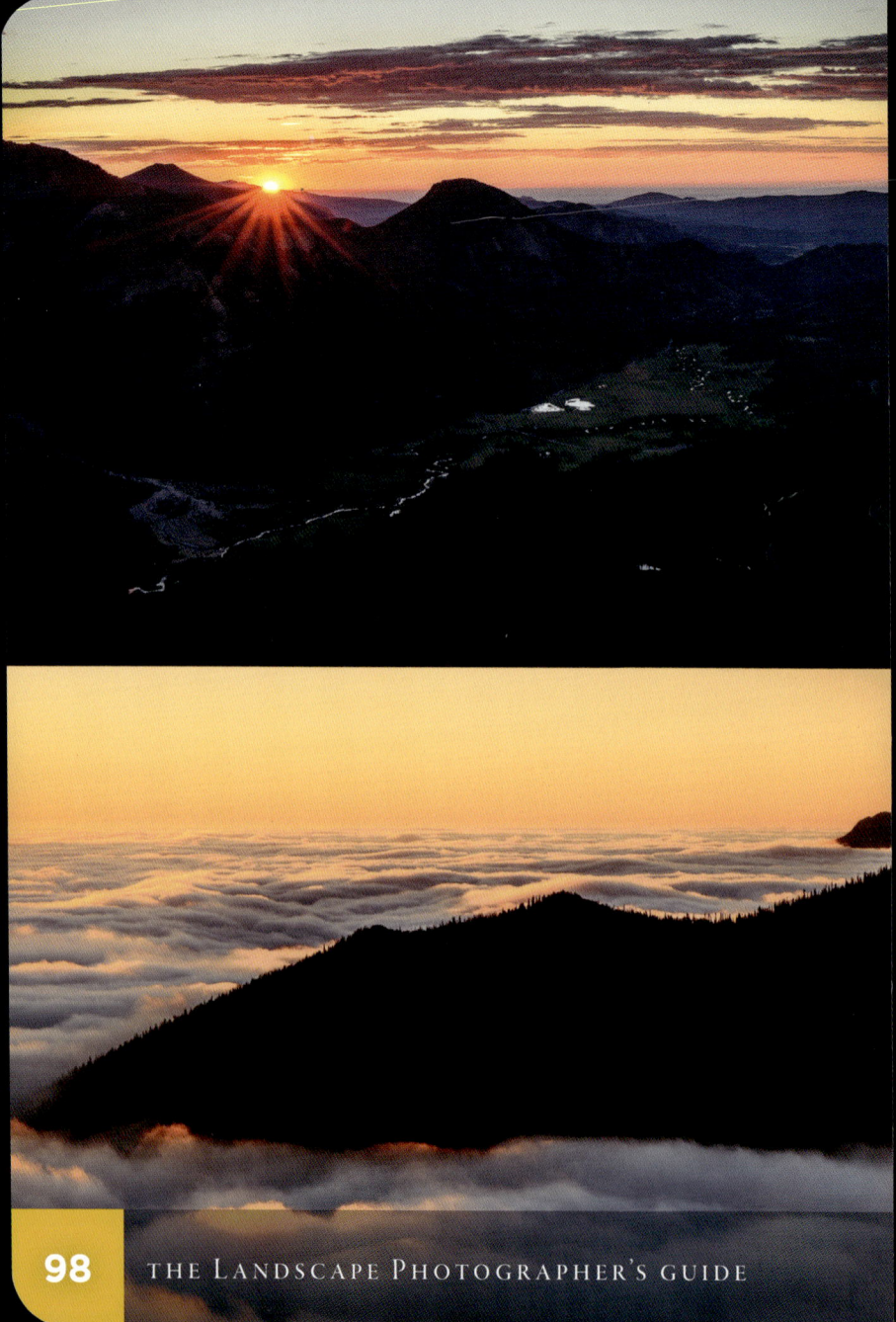

THE LANDSCAPE PHOTOGRAPHER'S GUIDE

the images.

The first of these locations is Many Parks Curve, located about a mile after Trail Ridge Road begins its steep climb from Hidden Valley. You'll drive past the viewpoint and park in the parking area on the right. You can then walk back across to the viewing area. Here you will see Beaver Meadows, Moraine Park, Longs Peak, Twin Sisters, and much more from this high vantage point. At sunrise, you can capture Longs Peak as it glows in the morning light. In the evening, about an hour before sunset, you can photograph Twin Sisters over the meadows.

If you continue walking down to the lower parking lot, you will see an area on the east side where you can climb out onto the rocks and capture some stunning sunrise images. Try to include these rocks in the foreground and Deer Mountain in the background. If you capture it just as the sun is rising, you can create a really dramatic photo.

The second pull-over is Rainbow Curve, which is located another five miles up Trail Ridge Road at nearly 11,000 feet above sea level. Here you have amazing vistas over Horseshoe Park and out across the Colorado plains. This viewpoint also provides closeup views of the Mummy Range off to the north. This is one of the best spots in the park for seeing the sun as it appears over the horizon in the morning. It is also a great place to photograph break-ing storms. Although it is often quite cold and windy up here, this is one spot where you can enjoy a dramatic view from the warmth of your car.

UTE CROSSING

If I want a nice quiet place to photograph sunset, the Ute Trail is generally my go-to location. It is such a peaceful place to walk, especially on a summer evening. At Ute Crossing you can hike a section of the Old Ute Trail, which has been used for millennia by native peoples to cross the Continental Divide. The views from up here are inspiring and make you feel like you are on top of the world.

The start of the trail can easily be missed, since the parking area only holds a small number of vehicles. It is located on the south side of the road about two and a half miles above Rainbow Curve, just as the view opens up to the south. If there is no parking available, continue uphill for about 300 feet to another parking area. This higher parking area provides an inspiring sunset view of Longs Peak from the comfort of your car.

From the Ute Crossing Trailhead, hike up the rocky hill and soon you will be rewarded with a dramatic perspective of Longs Peak. From here you can use a long lens to photograph Longs Peak as the sun sets. A longer lens will make the mountain look even more imposing.

If you have the energy and a head lamp, continue for another two miles to Timberline Pass, which is where the trail descends steeply into the valley below. At Timberline Pass you will find some of the best views of Longs Peak with lots of great rocks around to use in the foreground. There is almost no place more peaceful than this to enjoy a sunset in Rocky.

When hiking in the tundra, try to stay on the trail, as the tundra is very delicate. Many of these plants only have a 40-day growing cycle each year; any damage caused by feet can take hundreds of years to regenerate.

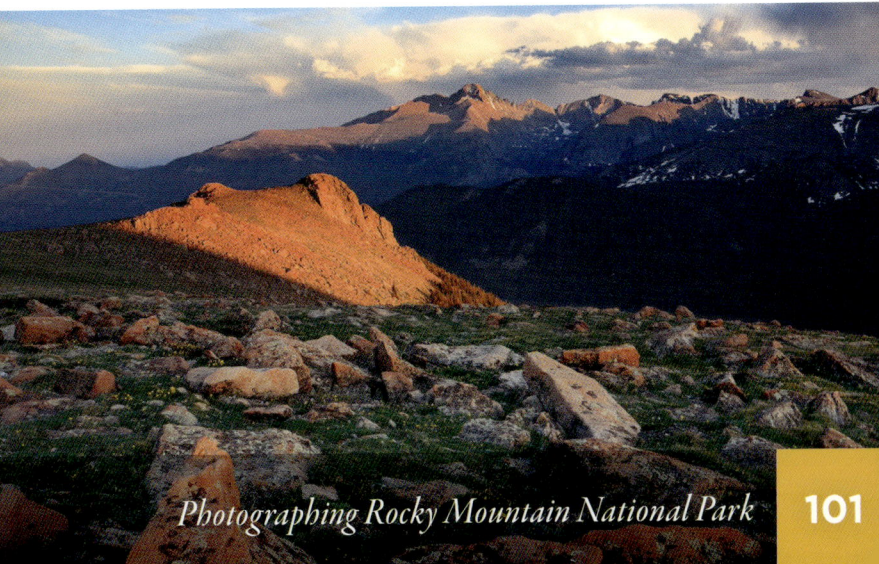

Photographing Rocky Mountain National Park

ROCK CUT

Rock Cut is probably the most popular place for photographers on Trail Ridge Road and is also one of the most visited places in Rocky Mountain National Park by the general public. It provides breathtaking views in all directions and gives one an understanding of the world above tree line. Making it particularly attractive to photographers is the fact that it is one of the few locations in the park where there are good options for shooting at both sunrise and sunset.

Rock Cut is located sixteen miles west of the Beaver Meadows Entrance on Trail Ridge Road. It is easy to know when you are arriving at Rock Cut, as the road passes through a narrow cut in a wall of rock. The parking area is located immediately after you pass through this gap.

The most popular image people take from Rock Cut involves photographing Longs Peak at sunset through a rock frame that almost seems to have been created with photographers and painters in mind. To reach this spot, follow the stone wall on the south side of the road to the east end of the parking lot. Then cross over to the other side of the stone wall and continue east up the rocks for about thirty feet. You will then be in the zone. The rock that is bent on top is called "the Thumb." As you create

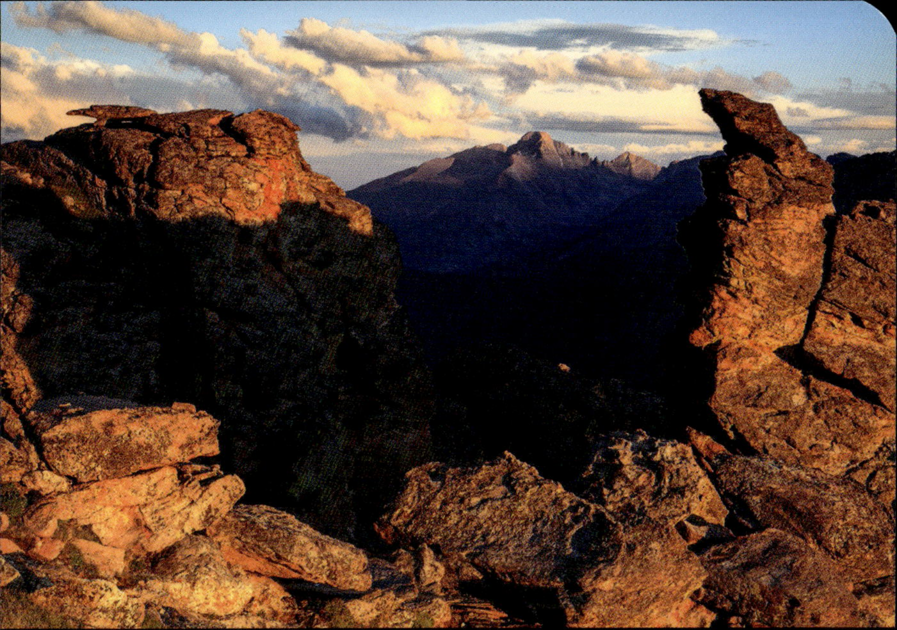

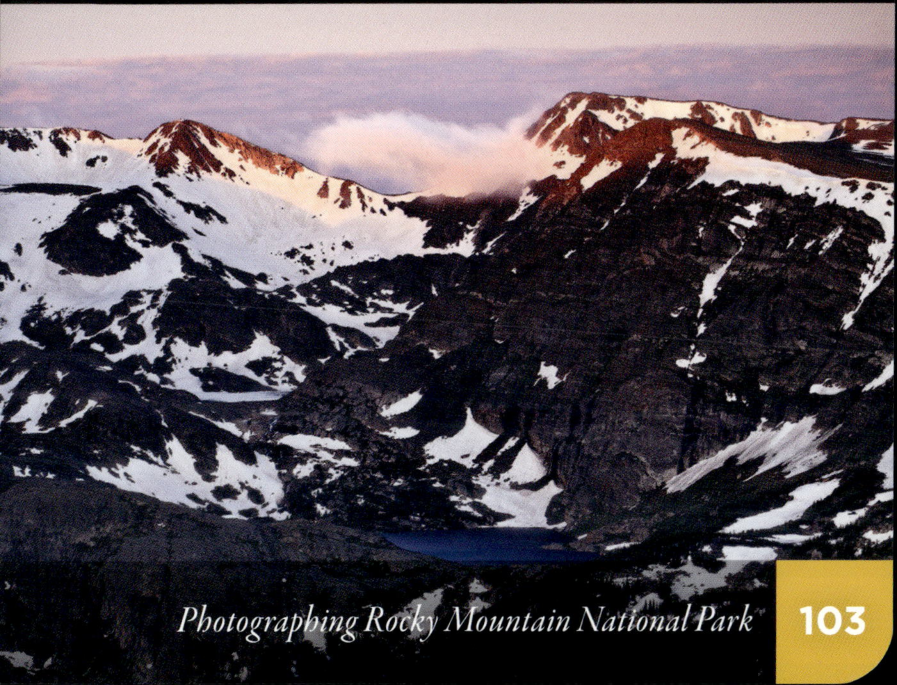

your composition, consider placing the Thumb just to the right of Longs Peak so it is sort of pointing toward the peak. As the sun sets during the summer, these rocks typically glow beautifully, as does Longs Peak. After photographing sunset, stick around for another ten minutes as the clouds above Longs Peak often turn pink about that time.

Another option is to stand on the south edge of the road and photograph the Gorge Lakes to your south. You will see one or perhaps two beautiful mountain lakes, but there are actually nine lakes in that region. This area can be photographed at both sunrise and sunset. While you are standing on the south side of the road, look over the wall and you will often find marmots playing at its base. In the evening you can also stand here and capture the sun setting behind the Never Summer Mountains.

Alternatively, follow the Tundra Communities Trail all the way to the end and you will find several views of Longs Peak as well as the Never Summer Mountains. About halfway up this trail you will also find one of the only hoodoos to be found in Rocky Mountain National Park. During the summer large herds of elk can often be seen grazing just off of this trail. Another photo option is right at your feet. Get down low on the trail and take macro shots of the fascinating tundra plants just off the trail. Do your best not to damage any of these delicate plants.

GORE RANGE OVERLOOK & AVC

Gore Range Overlook on Trail Ridge Road lies near the highest point on the road and affords great views up Forest Canyon and across toward the Never Summer Mountains. If you look closely, on a clear day you can even spot the Gore Range to the southwest, which is over fifty miles away. This is where the name for this overlook comes from.

If you want to photograph a snowy range of mountains bathed in the warm morning light, then be here at sunrise. This is one of the best places from which to photograph the Never Summer Mountains. What I particularly enjoy is the way the tundra grass lights up as it stretches out toward the mountains during the first twenty minutes of sunrise.

The sunset from here can also be spectacular as the sun dips behind the mountains, sometimes creating a wonderful silhouette while illuminating the clouds above with a dozen shades of red and orange.

Besides shooting toward the Never Summer Mountains

in the west, you can also face east from here and enjoy a very nice view of Longs Peak. This is one of the few spots in the national park that works well for photographing both sunrise and sunset. Keep your eyes open and you may even see me up there.

One of the nice things about this location is that even if the winds are howling and it is terribly cold, you can stay inside your vehicle and wait until the light is just right before stepping outside, since the best place to photograph is right next to your car.

While you're in the area, you can also drive down to the Alpine Visitor Center (AVC), which is just a few minutes down the road. Stop in to get a snack or to photograph the marmots that live just below the viewing wall. Once in a while, this can also be a good location to photograph at sunrise. I would want low clouds with a crack on the eastern horizon in order to have the drama needed to make this spot work.

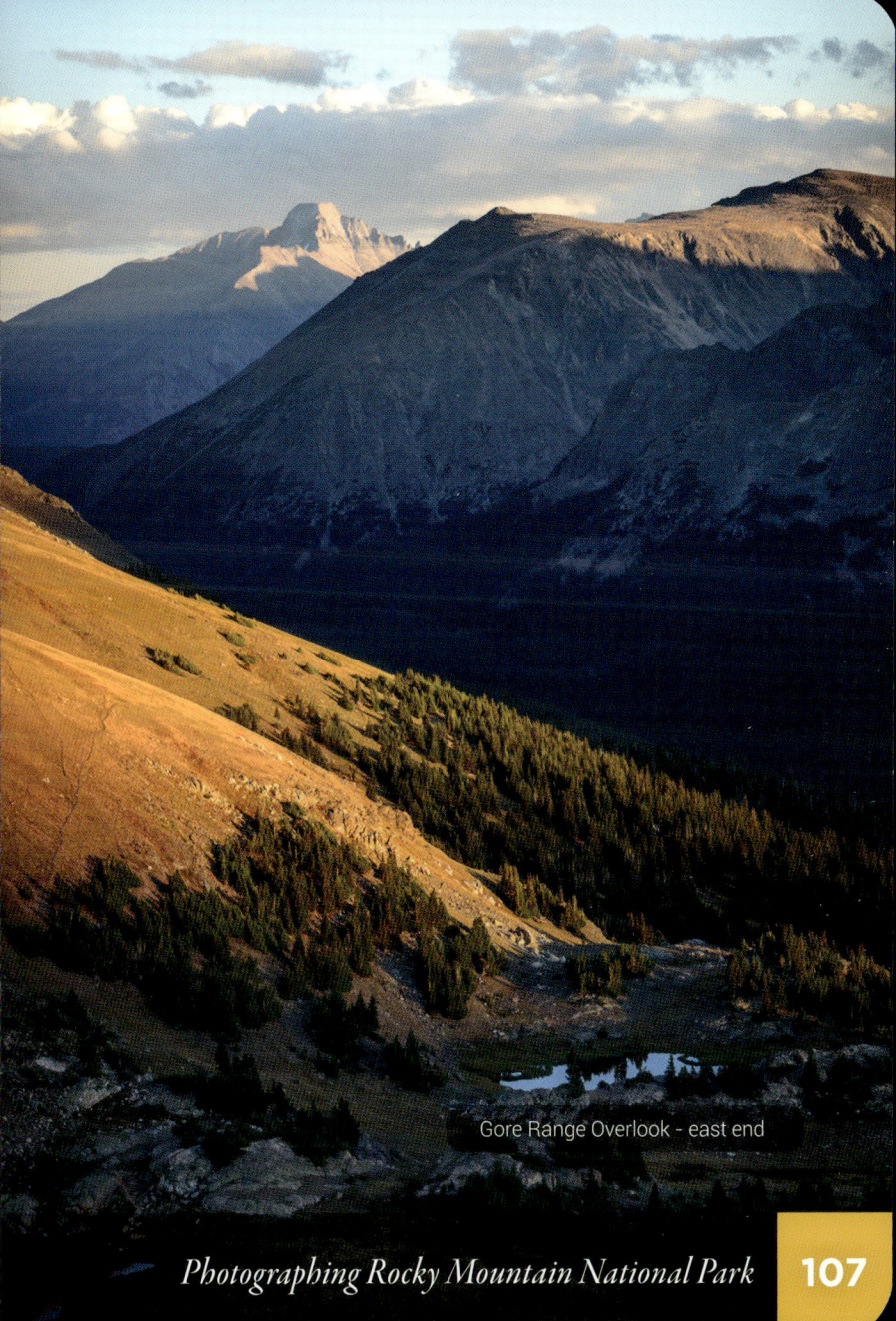

Gore Range Overlook - east end

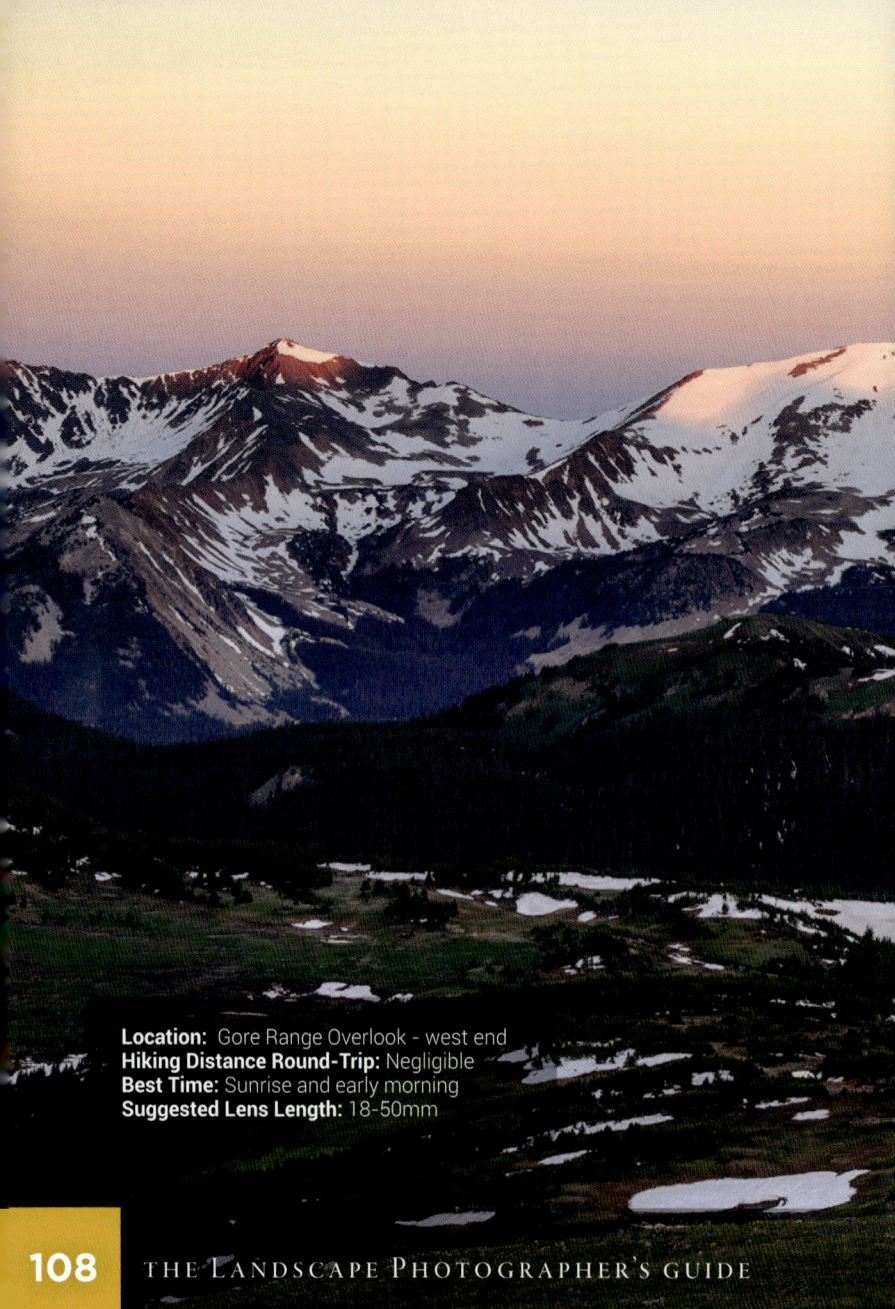

Location: Gore Range Overlook - west end
Hiking Distance Round-Trip: Negligible
Best Time: Sunrise and early morning
Suggested Lens Length: 18-50mm

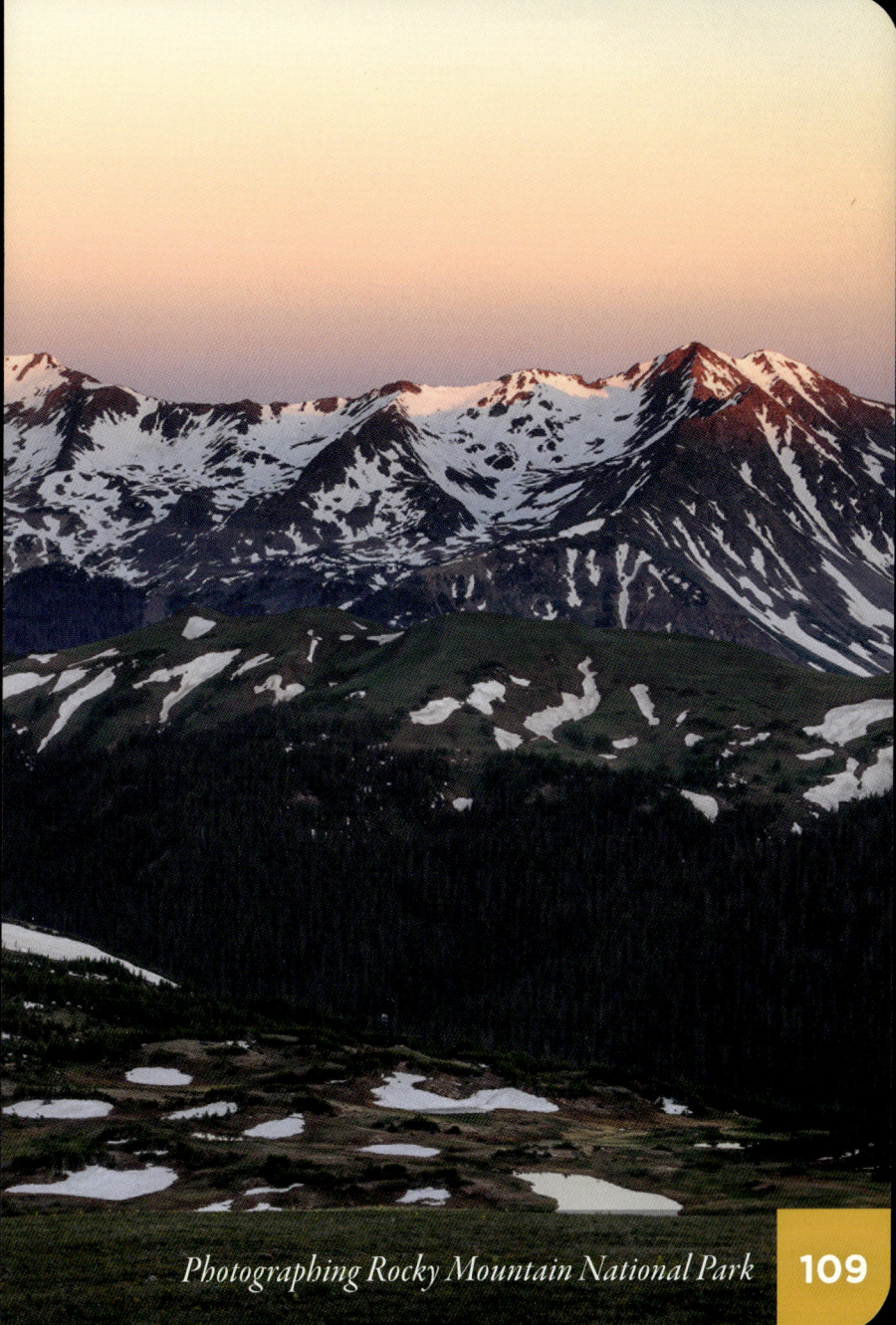

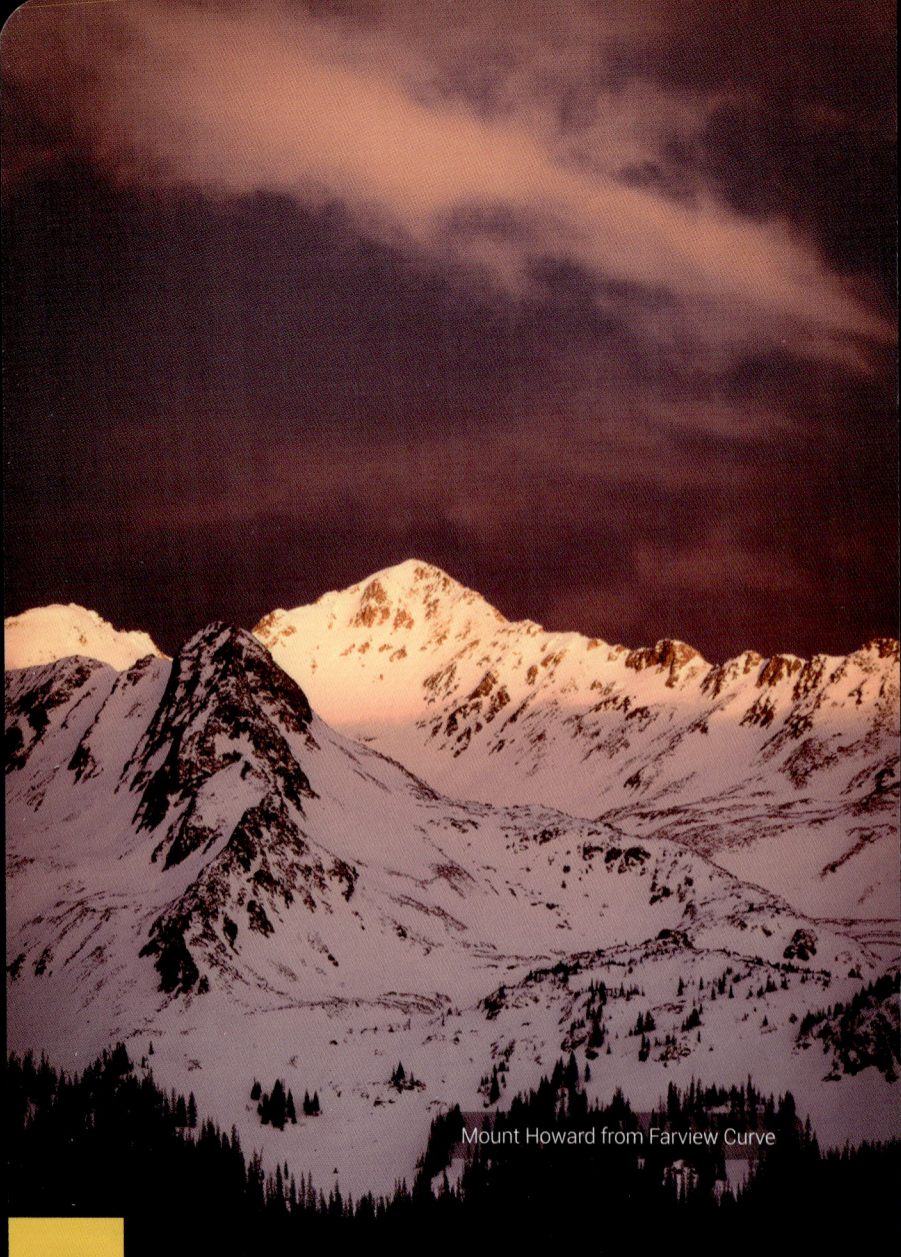

Mount Howard from Farview Curve

THE LANDSCAPE PHOTOGRAPHER'S GUIDE

FARVIEW CURVE

As you head west from the Alpine Visitor Center on Trail Ridge Road, it begins its descent by passing Poudre Lake and the Continental Divide. Poudre Lake is a beautiful stop but really only makes for great photographs under unique lighting and weather conditions. The road continues its steep descent before the vista opens up at Farview Curve; it's worth spending a few minutes here if you can find a parking spot.

Farview Curve can provide some very attractive images, particularly at sunrise or in the hour following sunrise. Typical of most overlooks, the photographic options from here are quite limited, as they lack foreground elements to help lead the eye into the photo. Nonetheless, you will find a great view of Red Gulch and the Never Summer Mountains.

By using a long lens between 100–300mm, you can isolate sections of the mountains to create a variety of compelling scenes. I find that this view is best during the spring when there is snow on the peaks to help give them definition.

On some summer mornings, you can look down from here onto the Kawuneeche Valley, where often you will find fog gently floating over the valley. This can also provide some very nice images, though they will feel a bit like they were taken from an airplane, since the valley floor is so far below.

KAWUNEECHE VALLEY

The Kawuneeche Valley takes its name from the Arapahoe word for "coyote." It is a beautiful valley that stretches most of the length of the western side of the park and is nourished by the mighty Colorado River that begins just a few miles north of the valley.

This lush valley is home to herds of elk and also to a large number of moose, so make sure you keep your eyes open as you travel its length. Be especially watchful for them on the roads at the beginning and end of the day. They often appear when you least expect it.

The first place you want to stop in the Kawuneeche Valley is the Beaver Ponds Overlook. It is not only a great place to spot moose but also a good place to shoot Mount Nimbus reflecting in the water at sunrise. The Beaver Ponds are located about a mile south of the Colorado River Trailhead, which is where Trail Ridge Road finally flattens out after its long descent from the tundra. The ponds are at the second dirt pull-over on the right.

The next place you should stop is the area I call the

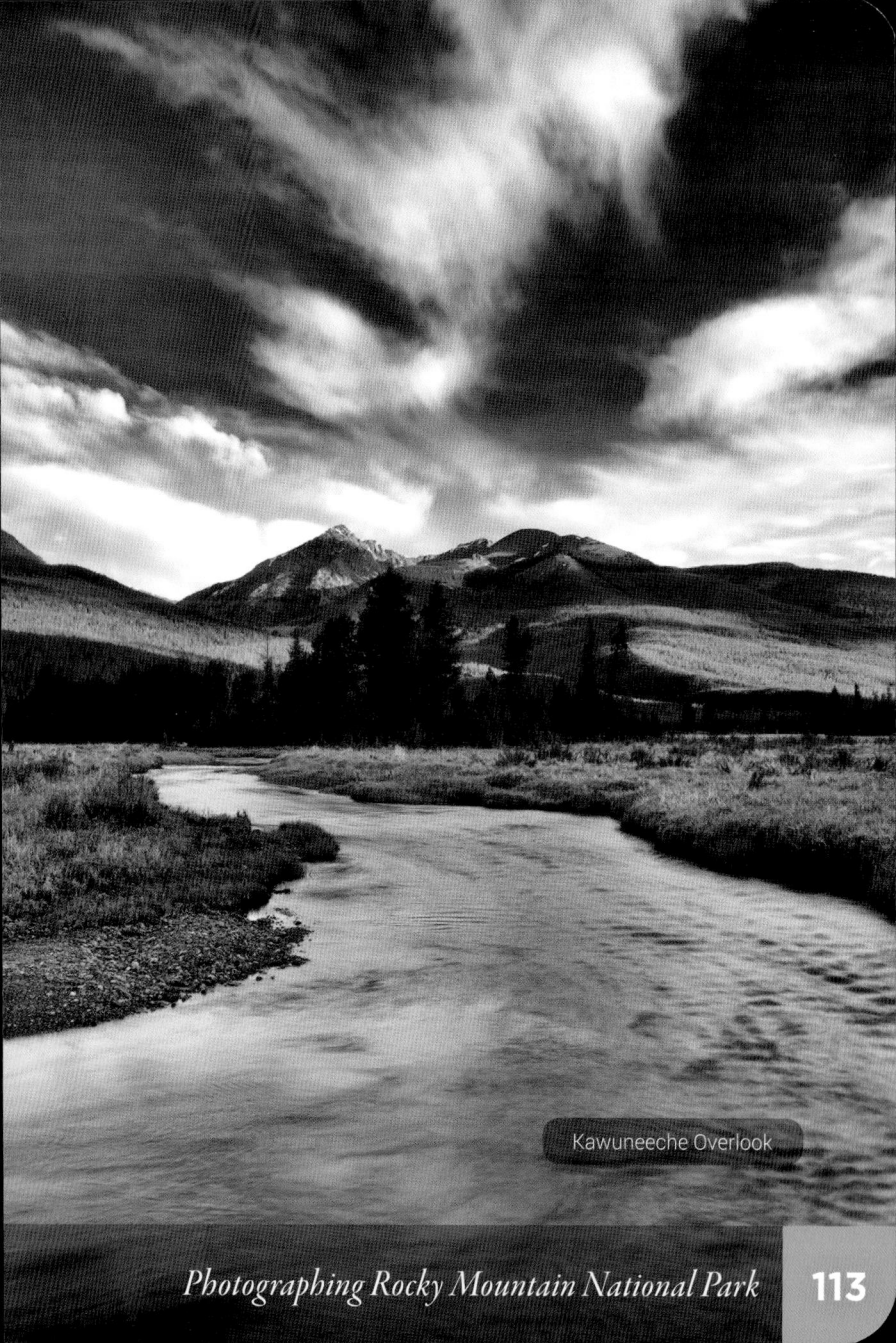

Kawuneeche Overlook

Kawuneeche Overlook. It provides great views of the Colorado River, the Kawuneeche Valley, and the Never Summer Mountains. This is perhaps the most classic shot to be had on the west side of the park. To find this location, drive south on Trail Ridge Road. When you pass the turn for the Coyote Valley Trail, continue for about half a mile and then look for a dirt maintenance road on your left. This is where you will want to park. Be certain to keep the road clear to allow park service vehicles to pass. Simply cross the road and look to the northwest, where you'll see a terrific view of Mount Baker and Mount Stratus over a turn in the Colorado River. The shot can be done right from the side of the road; however, expect a lot of cars to stop and ask you if you see a moose! This view is generally best from sunrise through midmorning and is a great spot all year round.

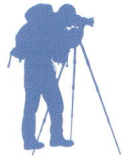

GRAND LAKE AREA

At the far-southwestern edge of Rocky Mountain National Park lies the little town of Grand Lake. From here there are several wonderful access points into the park that should not be missed.

EAST INLET

Often overlooked is the East Inlet Trail. Beginning on the far-eastern edge of Grand Lake, this trail follows the East Inlet all the way up to the Continental Divide and offers many photographic possibilities.

From the trailhead, take a gentle 0.3-mile stroll up to Adams Falls. This is a powerful waterfall that runs through a narrow section of rocks. Your compositional options for photographing this waterfall are limited due to the protective railing around the main view-point. However, the best view to be had is from this official overlook. While it is possible to crawl over the barrier and descend the steep slope, the viewpoints from below are actually not much better. Even down at the very base where it looks as if there might be unique compositions, it really doesn't have much to offer. Also, by crawling over the barrier, you are contributing to erosion of the area and there is a real risk of tripping or slipping, with dire consequences. Use a normal lens to capture the top half of the falls as they go around an island of trees, or use a wider-angle lens to include more of the falls below the trees.

Continue up the trail past the falls and in about two-tenths of a mile it will open up into a large meadow. Right as it opens up you can get some beautiful shots of Mount Craig (known by locals as Mount Baldy) reflecting in the gentle East Inlet. This is a great location for shooting sunset as Mount Craig catches the last light of the day.

Continue on the trail for another mile and you will come to the first of two overlooks spaced just a few hundred feet apart. Both of these overlooks will give you a view of the East Inlet River winding its way

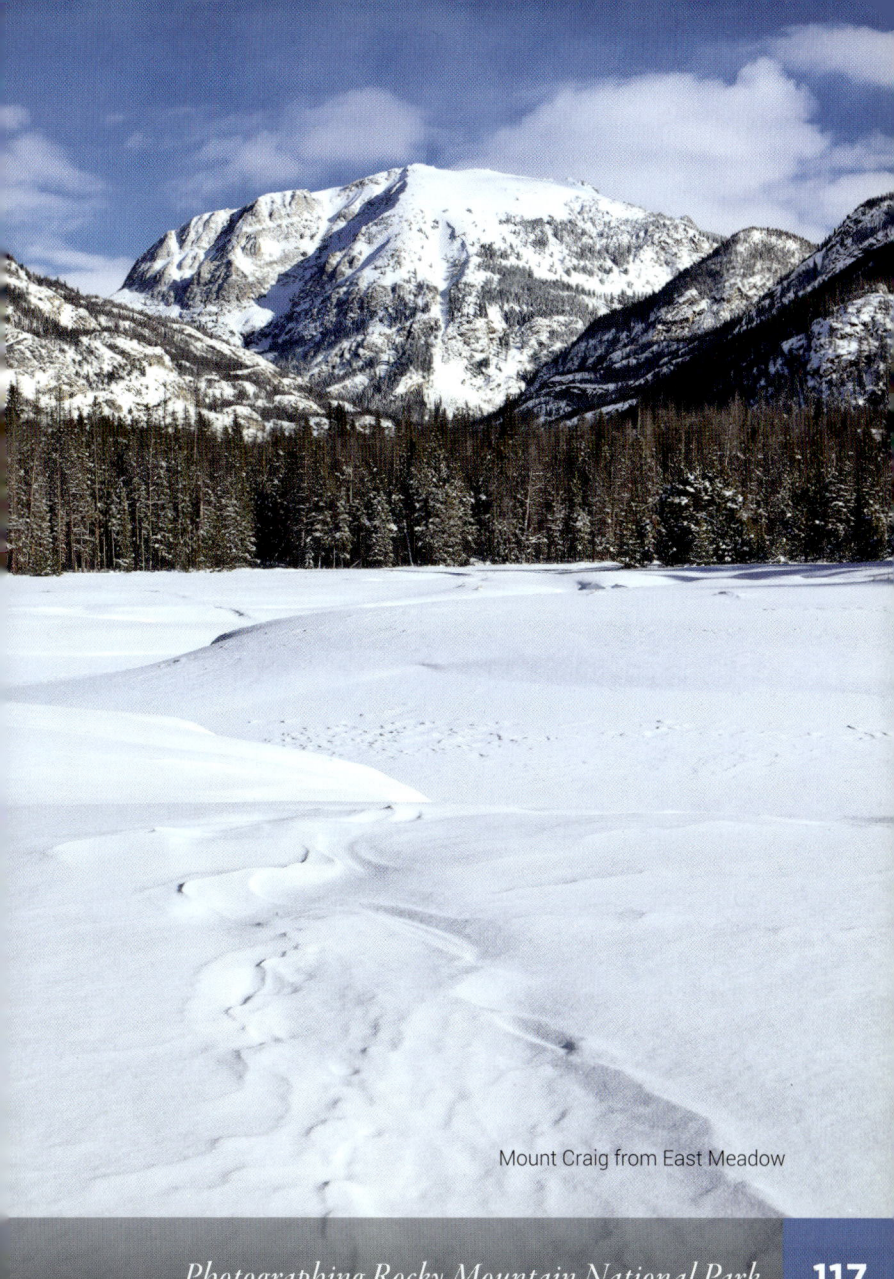

Mount Craig from East Meadow

through the meadow up toward Mount Craig. In my perspective, the first overlook provides the very best view to be found in East Meadow. It is best photographed in the hour leading up to sunset.

If you pay attention you may even see moose grazing in the meadow. They love the marshy terrain found here. Just be sure to give them plenty of space, as they can be quite dangerous and unpredictable.

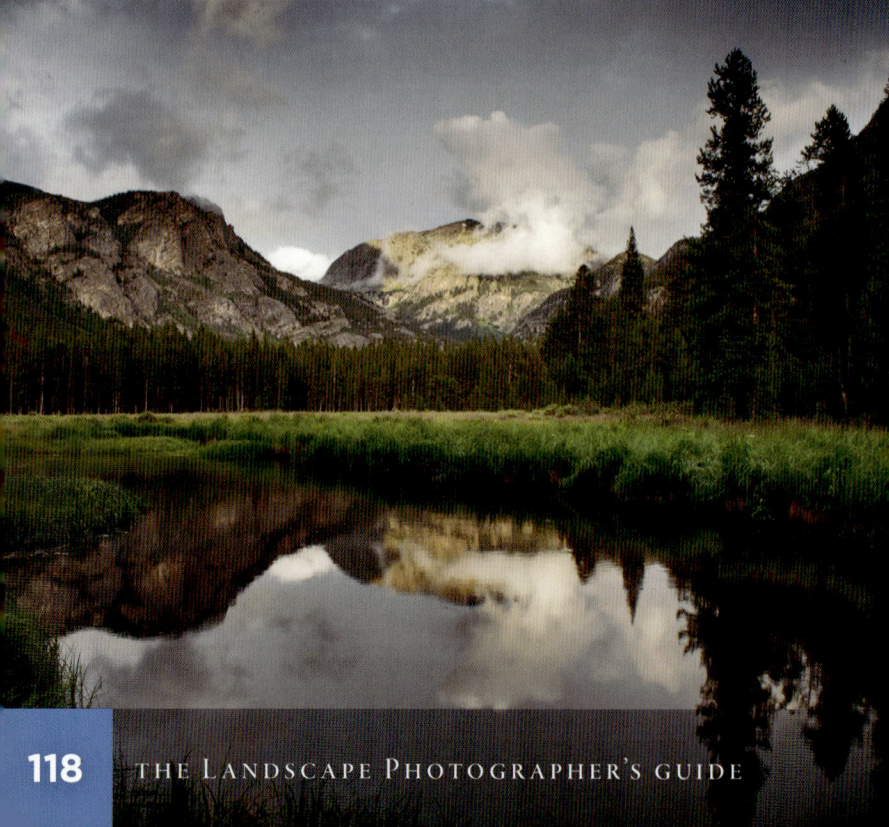

NORTH INLET

The North Inlet Trail begins on the north end of Grand Lake, just past Shadow Mountain Lodge. It is a long trail that continues all the way up to Flattop Mountain on the top of the Continental Divide. While there is much to see and photograph all along this trail, I'm only going to cover the first section, which is within easy access of the trailhead at Grand Lake. While this section of the trail does not provide any grand vistas, it is a great location for flower and wildlife photography.

The first section of the trail leads through a stretch of private property, so the trail is fenced on both sides for about three-quarters of a mile. Despite the fencing, there is often quite a bit to shoot along this stretch. In the summer, flowers line the trail, moose can often be found wandering nearby, horses are usually grazing behind the fence, and there are several areas where marmots can be seen wandering among the rocks. The best time to photograph this area is on an overcast day.

After the trail enters park property, it opens up into the peaceful meadow of Summerland Park with views of the North Inlet as it gently flows westward. The views to be found here are more intimate, including small segments of the river, flowers, and occasional wildlife.

It is one of the most peaceful places in Rocky. This area is generally at its best during June and early July when wildflowers are blooming along the sides of the path. The autumn can also be delightful when the aspen trees turn golden yellow.

Beyond the edge of Summerland Park, the trail begins to slowly climb upward. In about two miles it reaches Cascade Falls, a popular destination where you can watch the North Inlet dance down a steep boulder field. I find that this spot is best for closeup shots of various

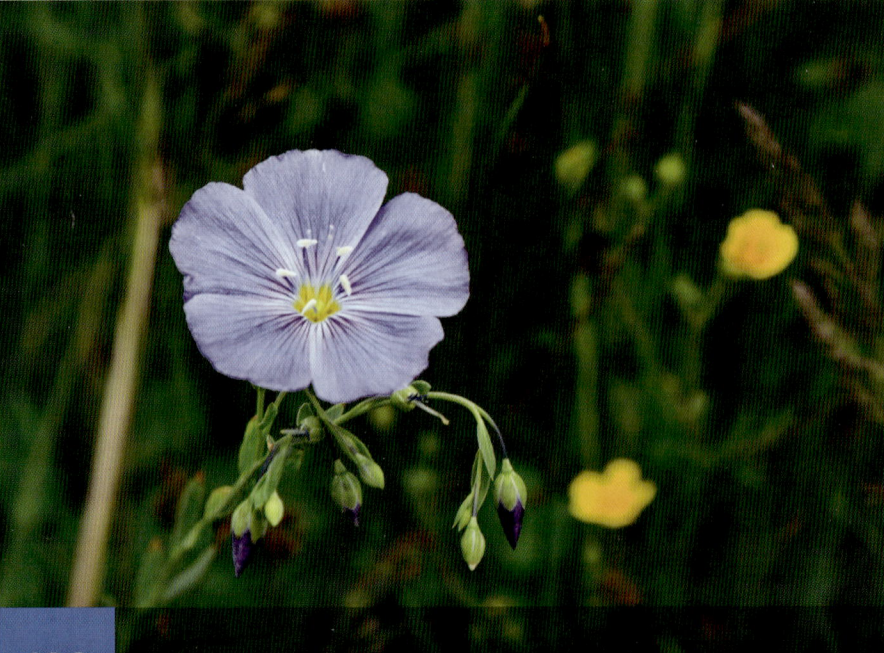

portions of the falls. Like most waterfalls and cascades, it is best photographed on an overcast day while using a slower shutter speed to help give it a sense of motion.

GRAND LAKE

Grand Lake is a cute little town with an Old West feel located on the western edge of Rocky Mountain National Park. Wooden boardwalks line the main street, while grassy parks and a lake full of sailboats invite people to come and relax. If you are on the west side of Rocky, then Grand Lake is worth a visit.

The main shot to be had from Grand Lake is of the lake itself with Mount Craig (Mount Baldy) towering in the background. There are several places to get such a view. One of the best locations is from Point Park on the west end of the lake. This is a great little park for picnics and has a clear view east over the lake. If you are here on a summer's day you may be able to include a sailboat or two in your image. You can also walk down to the bridge over the outlet to get a higher perspective of the lake.

You can also get a similar shot but with a bit more foreground from the bridge on Jericho Road, which is just a little farther west from Point Park. This view looks up the channel past a number of houses and their docks. While

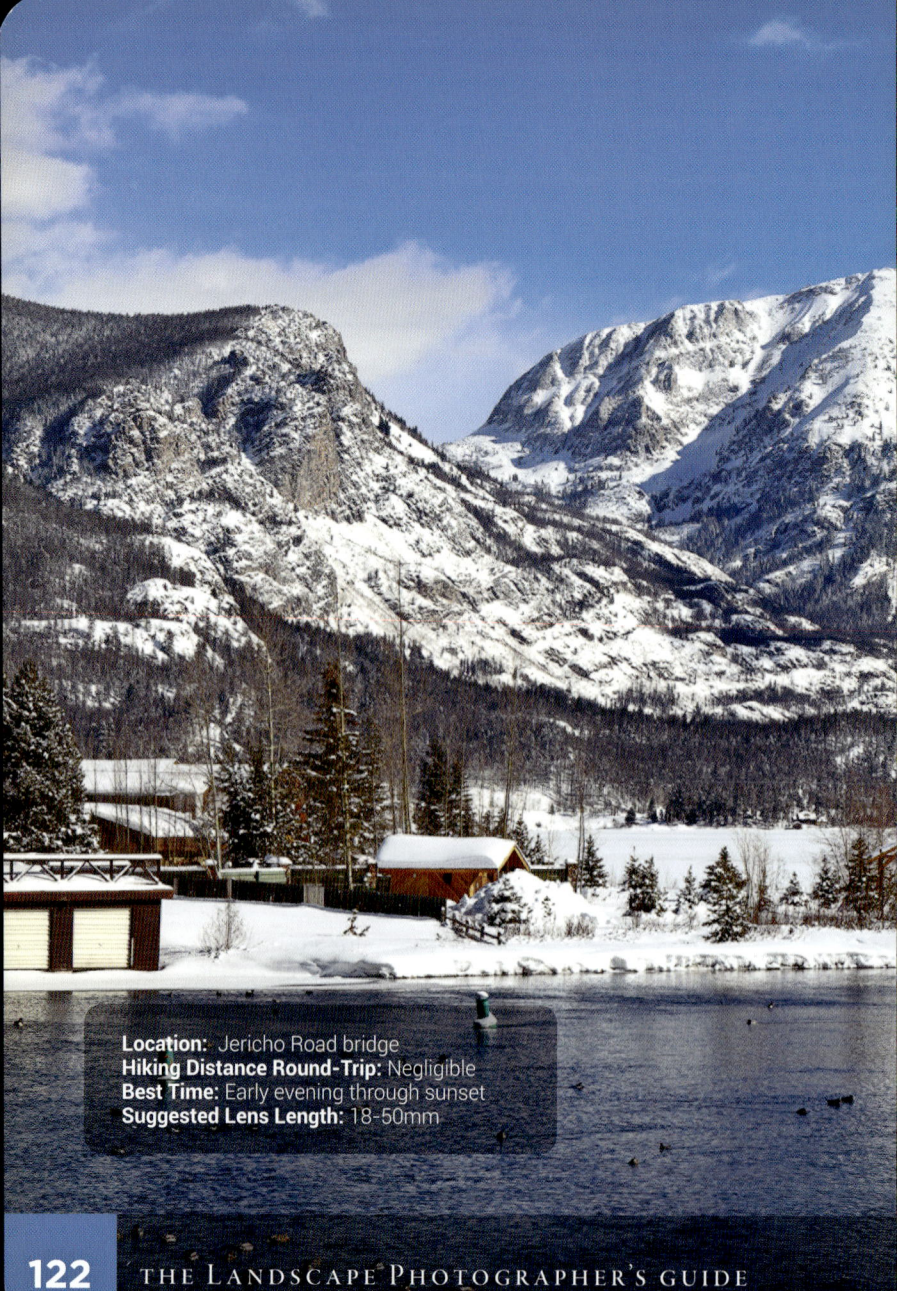

Location: Jericho Road bridge
Hiking Distance Round-Trip: Negligible
Best Time: Early evening through sunset
Suggested Lens Length: 18-50mm

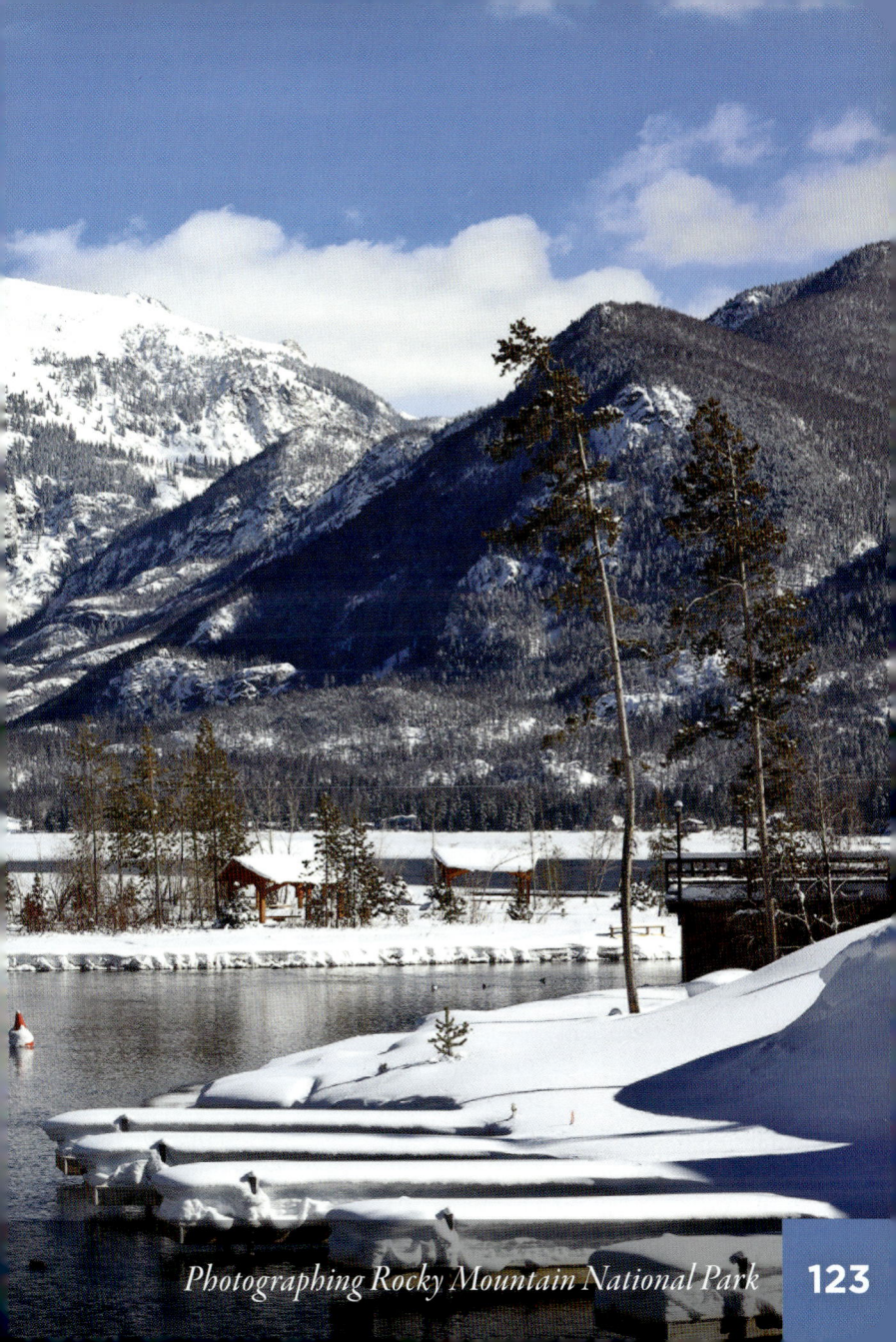

not necessarily a nature shot, it does give a good feel for Grand Lake.

A third location that provides excellent views of the lake is from Highway 34 half a mile south of where it intersects with the turn for Grand Lake. There is a large pull-over next to the Welcome to Grand Lake sign. It overlooks Shadow Mountain Lake with Grand Lake behind it and Mount Craig in the distance. This is one of my favorite views in the area.

The best time to photograph this direction is generally in the evening. Although it is a gorgeous shot all year round, I think it is at its most beautiful in early October.

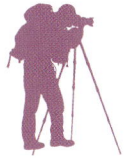

SEASONS

Each season of the year brings its own version of beauty. As the park travels through the year, the light and the foliage both change, providing new opportunities almost every week. Below I highlight some of the main things to keep in mind when photographing each season.

SPRING

Spring in the Rocky Mountains is not like spring in much of the rest of the United States. While most of the country is enjoying warm weather, green grass, and blooming flowers, Rocky is still cold and snow covered. In fact, its snowiest months of the year are in the spring. It is not uncommon to get big snows well into the month of May. As a result, spring is quite short and sometimes seems to be nonexistent.

Usually around the second week of April we begin to see the ice thawing on some of our lakes. This can provide great reflection opportunities with floating ice, creating scenes that you won't be able to find at other times of year. The grass in the lower meadows will still be brown, but you may be able to find a few pasqueflowers blooming under large ponderosa trees. The south side of Lily Lake, Wild Basin just to the south of the dirt road, Tuxedo Park, and the first half mile of the Deer Mountain Trail are all good places to look for pasqueflowers from mid-April through early May.

In mid-May, the meadows begin to turn green and the leaves begin to bud. The tundra, however, will still be brown and possibly snow covered. Around the end of May, Trail Ridge Road opens and allows access to a world that has been largely inaccessible for over six months.

In early to mid-June, you will begin to find flowers in the lower meadows. The meadow across from the Beaver Meadows Entrance Station, Moraine Park, and Beaver Meadows are all great places to capture scenes with a variety of flowers and snowy peaks. Make sure not to damage these delicate flowers so that they'll return the following year and others can enjoy them.

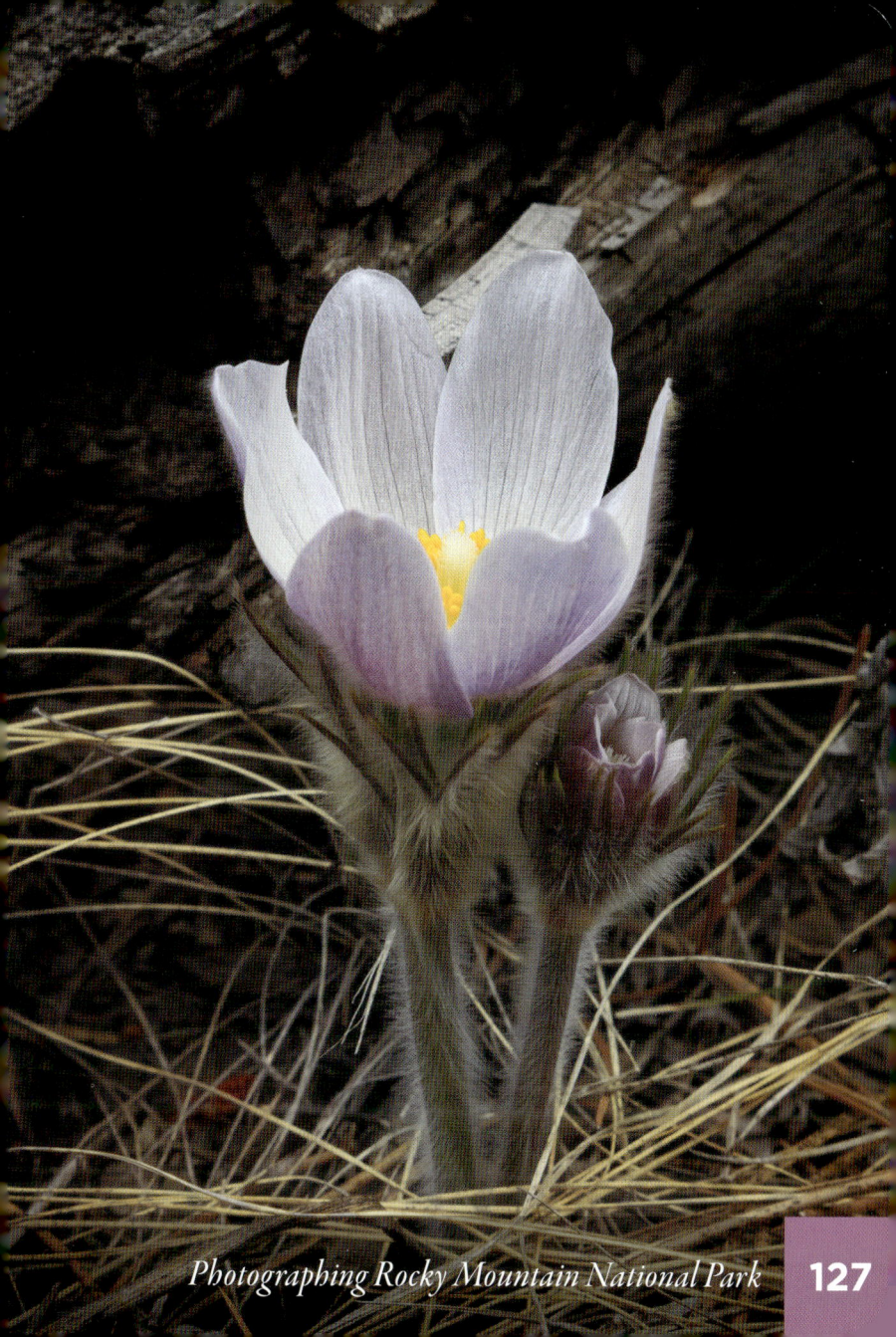

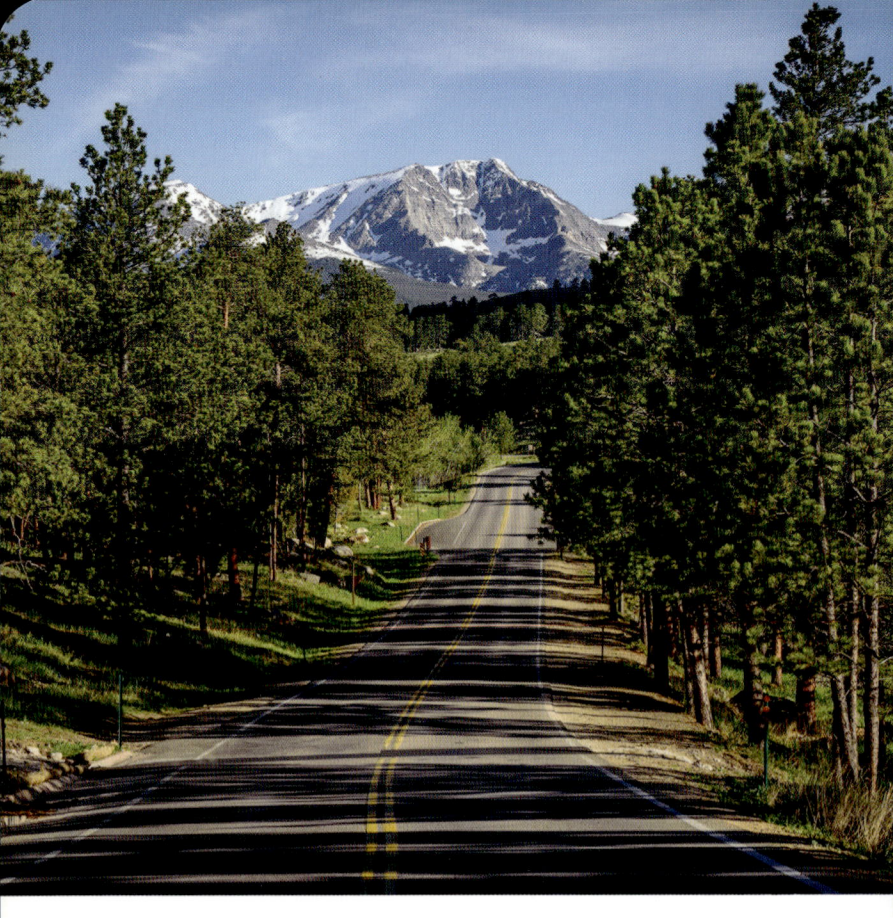

The weather in the spring can be quite unpredictable, but such weather also makes for great photographs. I find June to be one of my most productive months of the year, as it often has dramatic skies, lush foliage down below, and snowy peaks above.

SUMMER

Summer is the busiest time of year in terms of the number of visitors but is a wonderful time to photograph. The entire park opens up, providing the chance to visit some of the most stunning areas of the park that are difficult to reach during other times of the year. Summers are characterized by deep blue cloudless skies at sunrise and sunset, making photography a bit challenging, but there are often violent storms around 2–3 p.m. which can make for interesting photographs as the storms break. Just make sure you plan accordingly and aren't out on the open tundra during the storms!

In early summer, the meadows near the entrance stations are green and lush. You may find a large variety of flowers at this easy-to-reach location as well as in the other lower meadows. Higher up in the tundra along Trail Ridge Road, you will find that things are beginning to slowly change from brown to green. By this time, most of the lakes have lost their ice and have become great photographic locations. Rocky Mountain National Park has nearly 150 alpine lakes, so there are many to choose from.

Around the end of June or early July, wildflowers begin to carpet the tundra. This is a beautiful time to spend a while on the Ute Trail. At this time of year, the elk begin

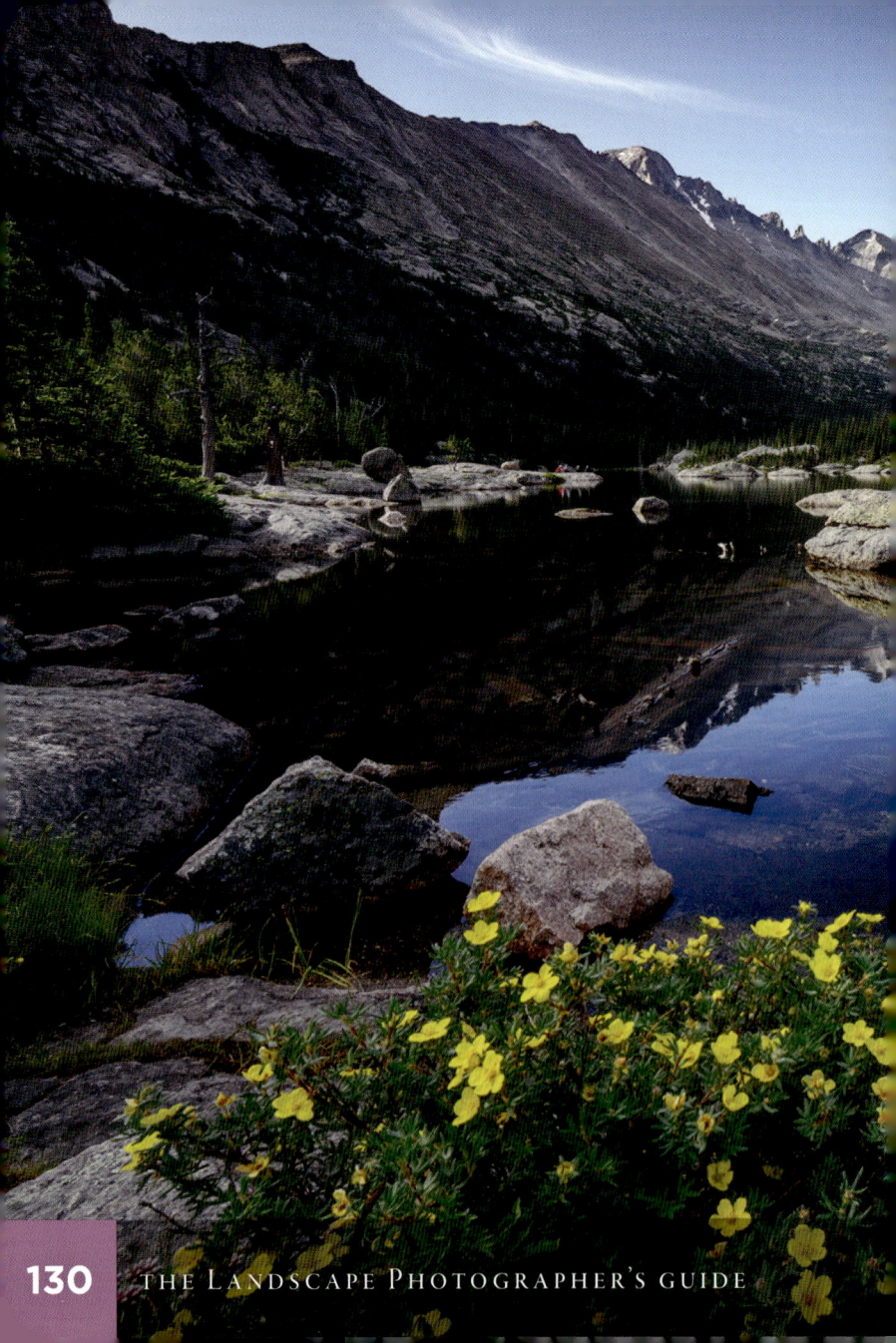

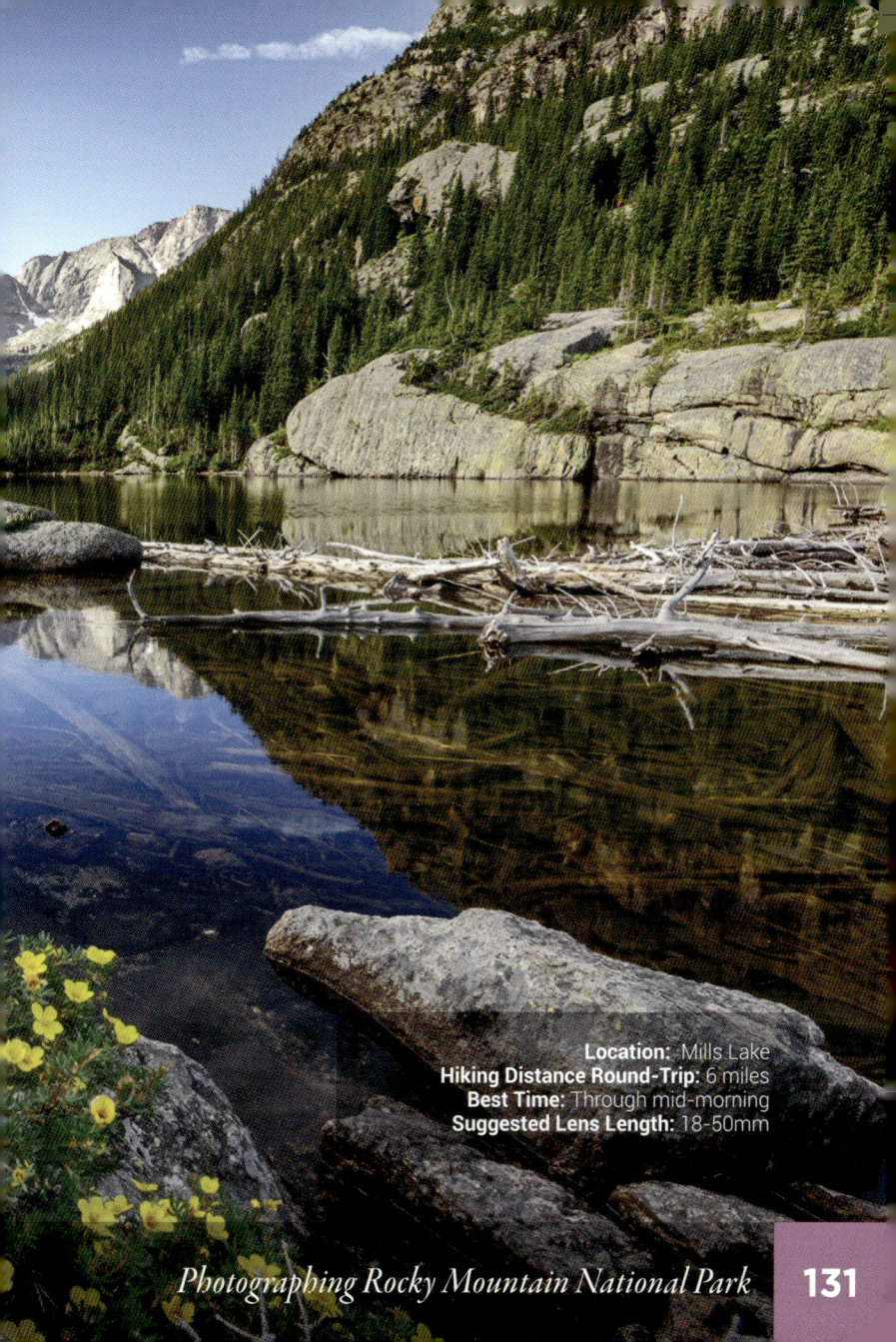

Location: Mills Lake
Hiking Distance Round-Trip: 6 miles
Best Time: Through mid-morning
Suggested Lens Length: 18-50mm

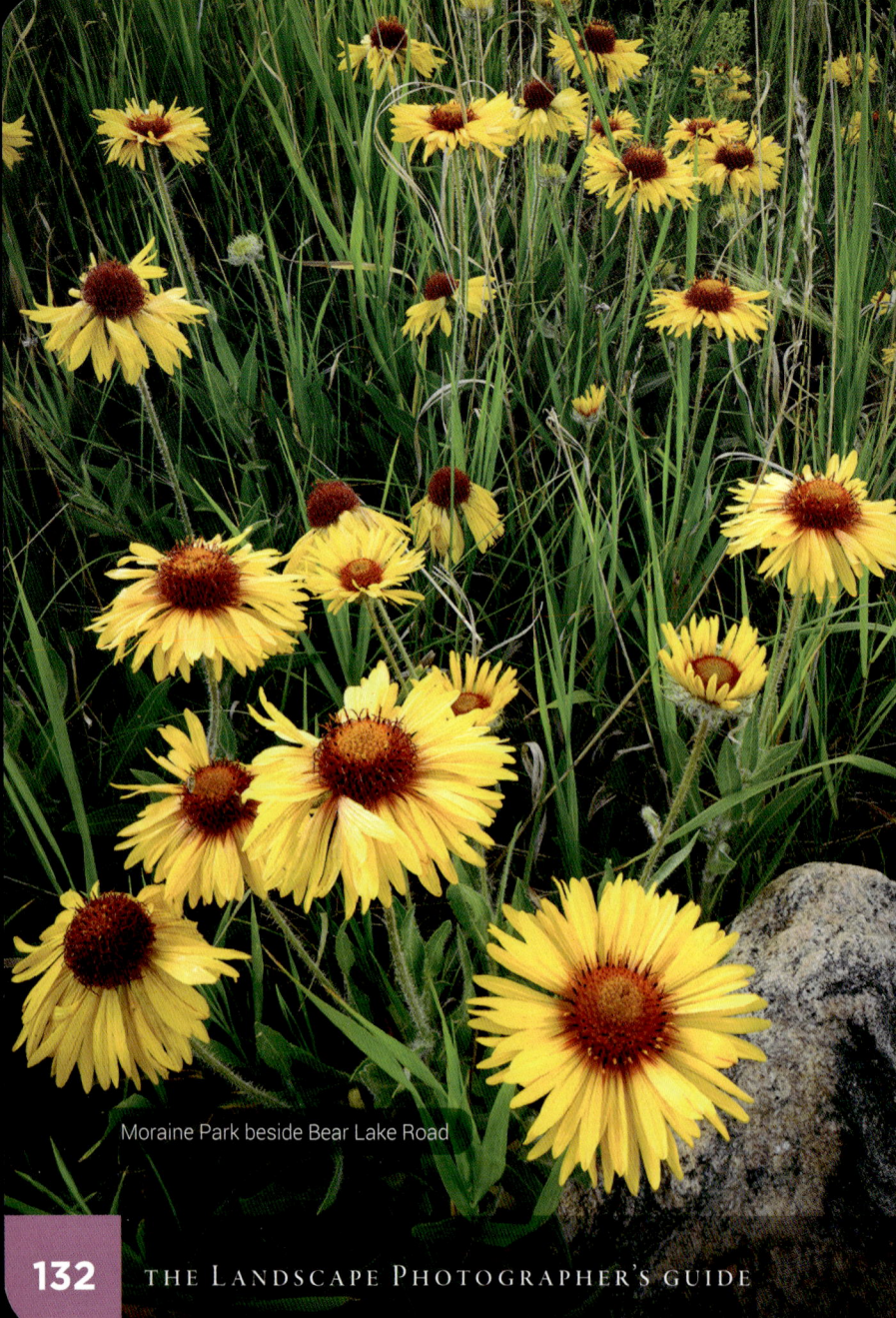

Moraine Park beside Bear Lake Road

to migrate to the tundra and can often be photographed with the rugged peaks in the background.

During the middle of summer, the sun will rise and set quite far to the north, so the best mountains to photograph are those that are facing north and will catch the colorful light of sunrise and sunset.

In August, the lower meadows begin to show the first indications of change as they take on some rust-colored hues. This is also the time that the tundra begins its transition to autumn. Its short-lived summer is quickly over and the alpine havens that flourish up high turn from green to a rich red color that can often be seen on hillsides from miles away.

AUTUMN

Although, it is a very delicate and fleeting time, autumn is perhaps the most beautiful time of year in Rocky Mountain National Park. High winds sometimes steal the show just as it is starting, so you never know what you will get or how long it will last. Below I have described the general pattern, but be aware that no year is ever truly typical.

Autumn in Rocky begins in the high country and slowly makes its way to lower elevations. From mid-August through mid-September, the autumn begins in the high tundra as plants and grasses take on orange and red hues. Not many people pay attention to what is happening higher up, but I think autumn in the tundra provides some amazing photographic options. Drive up Trail Ridge Road to enjoy the sights and get some closeup shots of the changing tundra. Bring a jacket, hat, and gloves, though, as it can start to get rather chilly at higher altitudes.

By the third week of September, the higher aspens, such as those at Bear Lake, begin to reach their peak color. Highway 7 on the east side of the park will also start to look really colorful. This third week of September is also about the time that the elk rut moves into full force and

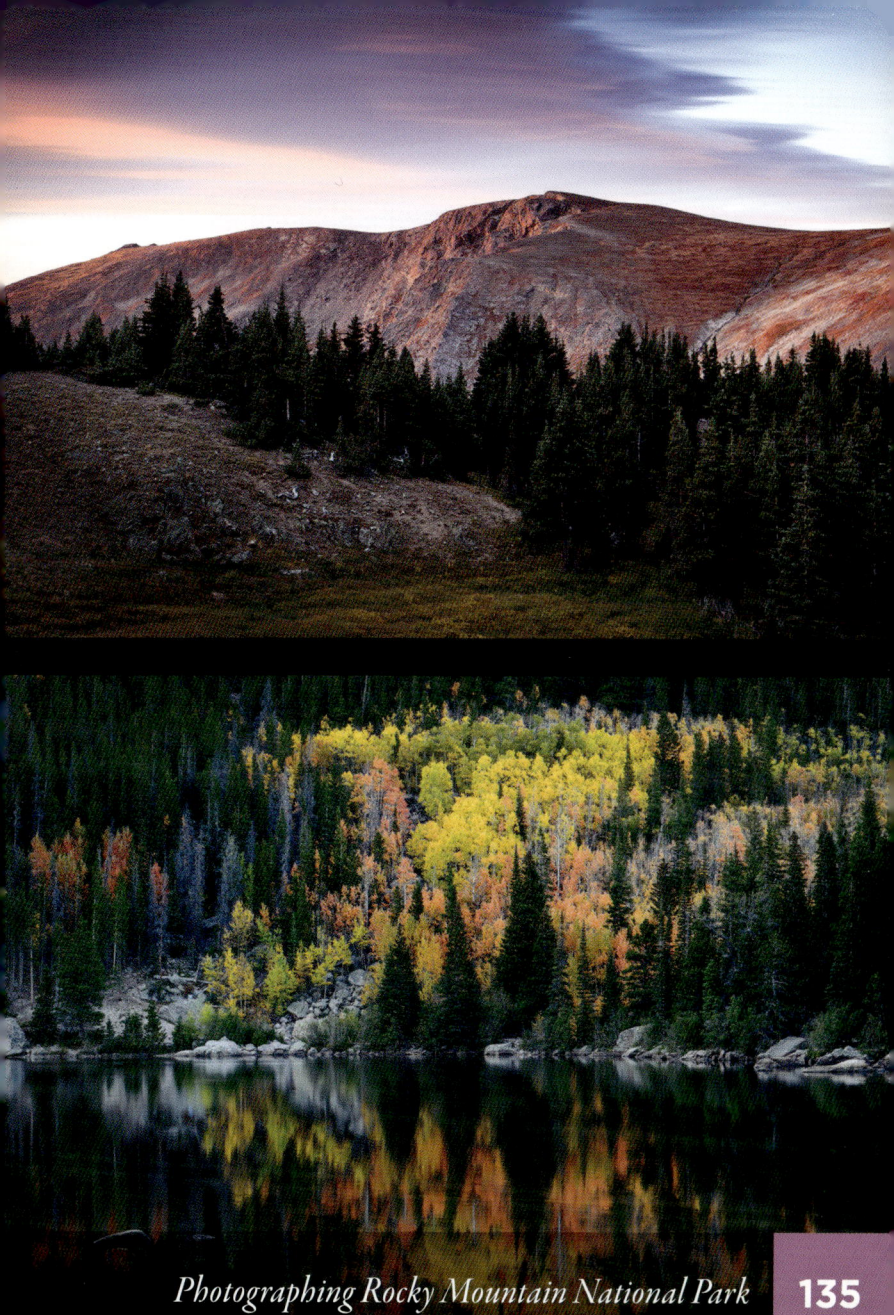

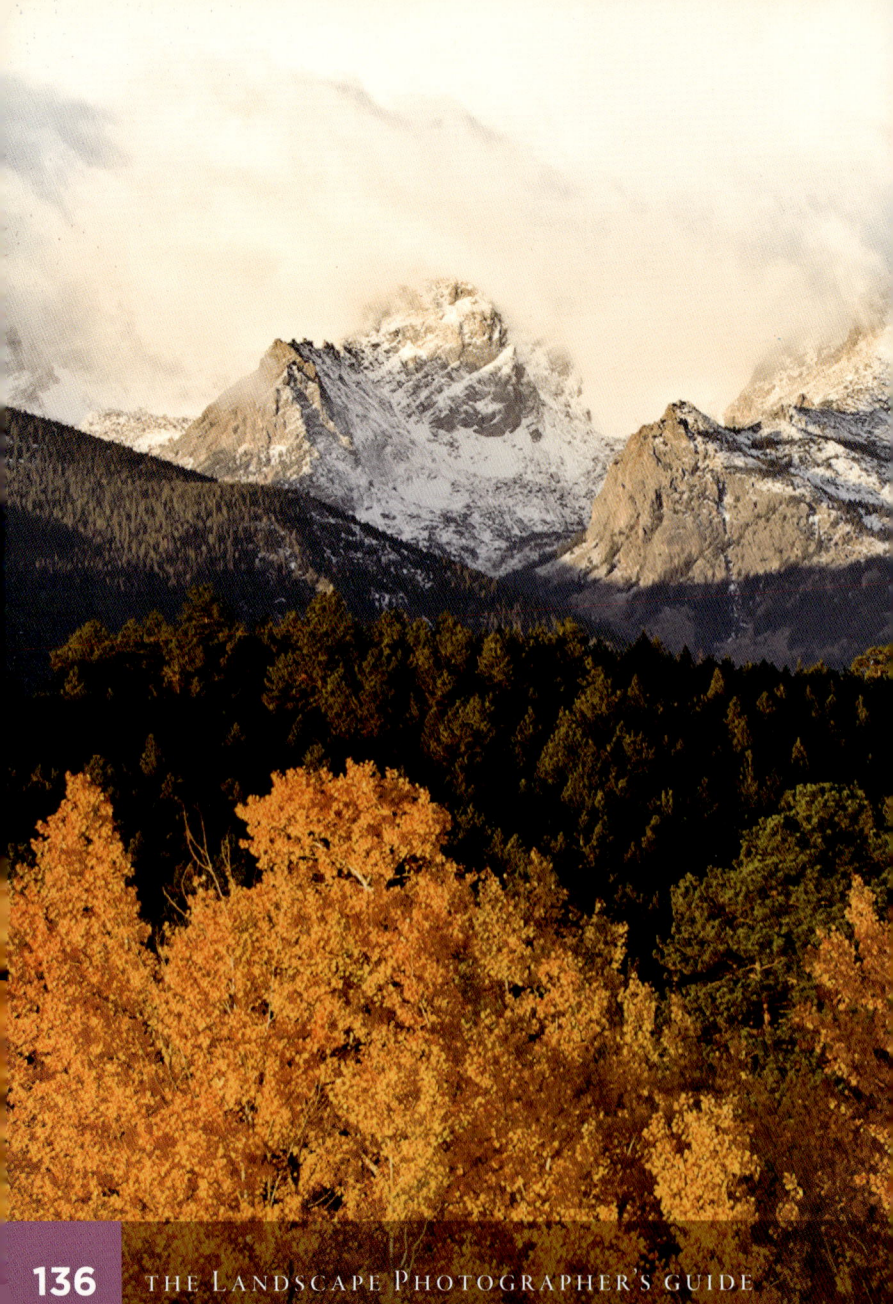

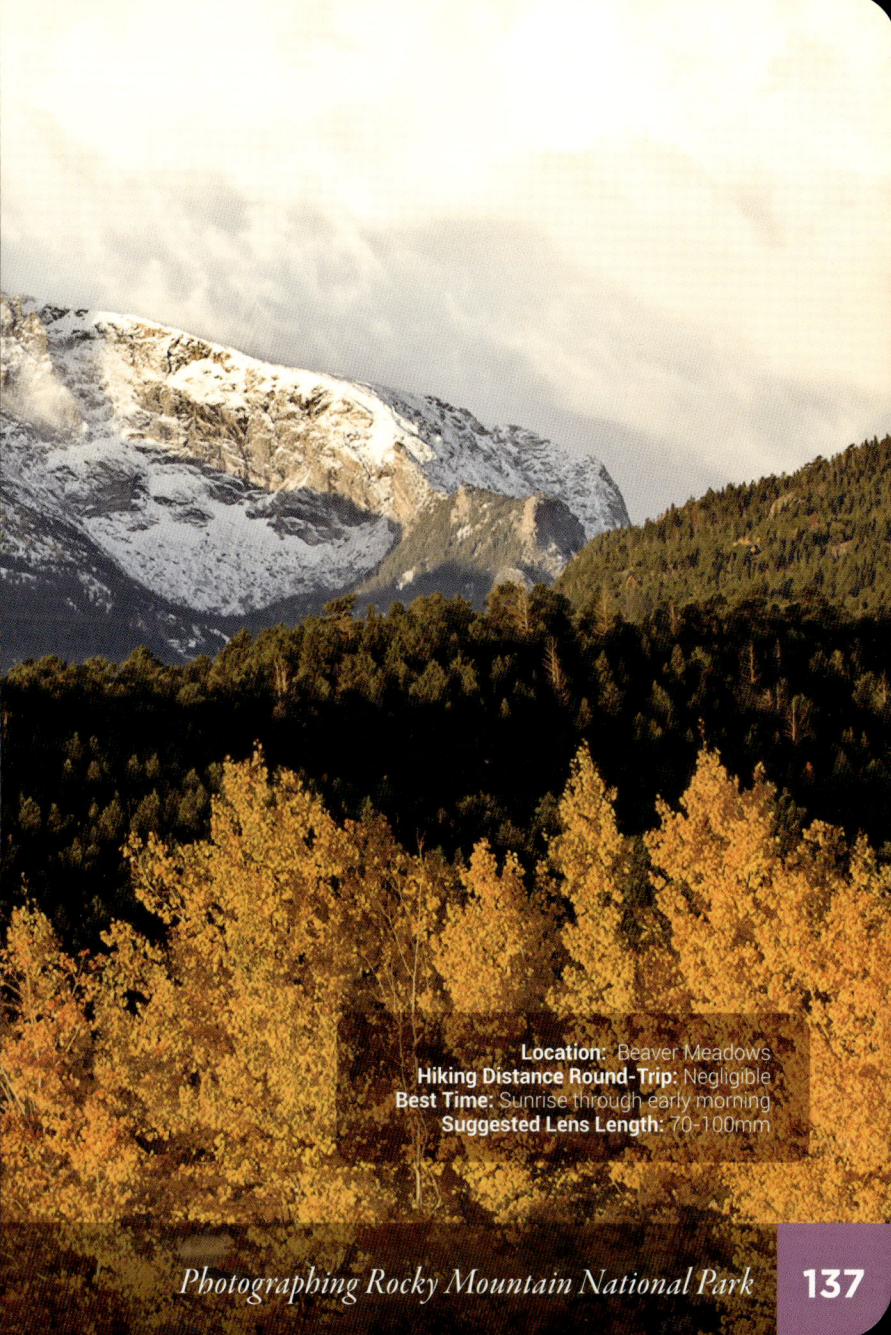

Location: Beaver Meadows
Hiking Distance Round-Trip: Negligible
Best Time: Sunrise through early morning
Suggested Lens Length: 70-100mm

Photographing Rocky Mountain National Park

the meadows are filled with the sound of bugling and the sight of majestic elk sparring. You can find them gathering in the lower meadows of the park.

During the fourth week of September, the colors at Bierstadt Moraine along Bear Lake Road should reach their peak and they are a magnificent sight to behold. You can get shots of these amazing fall colors from the Storm Pass Trailhead. Conditions should also still be good along Highway 7 and along the Kawuneeche Valley, though more limited.

Around the first week of October, the aspens in the lower meadows from Hollowell Park to Horseshoe Park begin to look their best. You'll find gorgeous groves of aspen in peak color in various parts of Moraine Park, on the way to Cub Lake, near the Beaver Meadows Entrance Station, in Upper Beaver Meadows, near the Alluvial Fan, and in many other areas at that elevation.

During the second week of October, the autumn colors are finishing up in the lower meadows, and the aspen trees around the town of Estes Park begin to reach their peak. Right around the fifteenth of October the final autumn color in Rocky begins to fade as trees quickly drop their leaves. The first snowfall usually seems to arrive around this same time as well.

WINTER

Winter is Rocky's longest season, with snow often arriving as early as mid-October and often continuing past April. It is also the windiest time of the year; it's not uncommon to have winds in the 30–50 mph range with even stronger gusts. Despite this, there are occasional times of reprieve when conditions are perfect for photography.

When the snowstorms arrive, they often bring a deep stillness with them. I suggest heading out just as soon as a storm ends. You may have a couple of hours of calm to photograph serene winter wonderland scenes during this brief period of time. The ideal storm is the one that ends just before sunrise so that you can get fresh snow on all the trees and rocks, which are then lit by the beautiful, warm morning light. The contrast makes for heavenly photos.

To travel around in the winter, I recommend using snowshoes and hiking poles, which can be rented throughout Estes Park for about $5 per day. I also recommend that you stay off of any steep slopes, as avalanches are a real danger during this time of year, even on well-known trails. Visit the Colorado Avalanche Information Center to find the latest avalanche conditions.

In the winter, it is all about playing with contrasts. Animals contrast very well with the white snow, as do blue skies, warm light, hikers in red jackets, etc. The photographic possibilities in the winter are nearly endless when the weather cooperates.

Most of the locations listed in this guide can still be accessed in the winter, although Trail Ridge Road is generally closed from mid-October until the end of May.

Keep in mind that during the winter the sun will be much farther to the south. The best mountains to photograph will be those that are south facing because these are the peaks that catch the warm morning and evening light.

The west side of the park is much more difficult to access due to the closure of Trail Ridge Road, but you can still get there by taking I-70 and then continue past Winter Park. The west side of Rocky generally gets much more snow than the east side and also less wind, so it can be a great area to photograph in the winter.

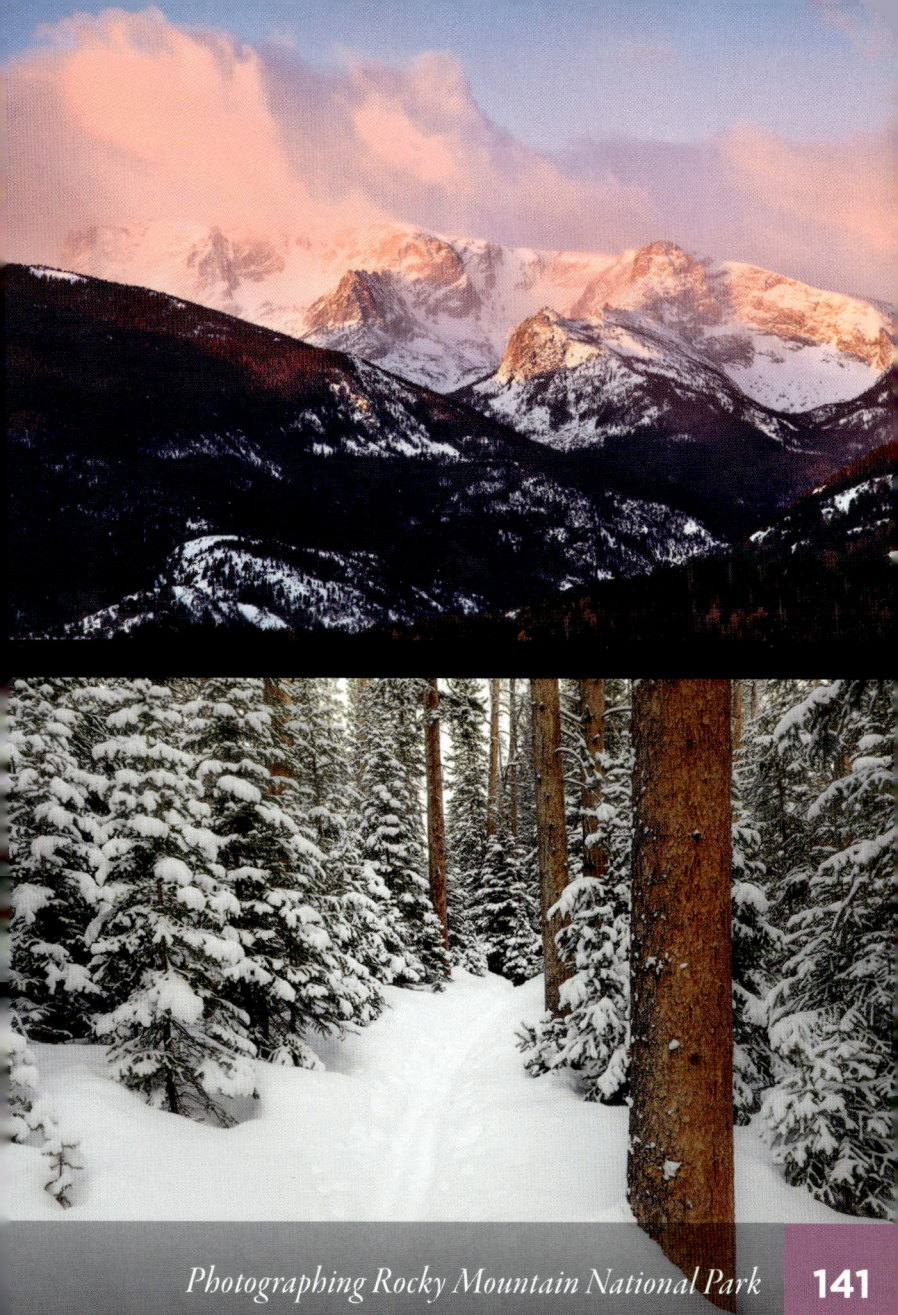

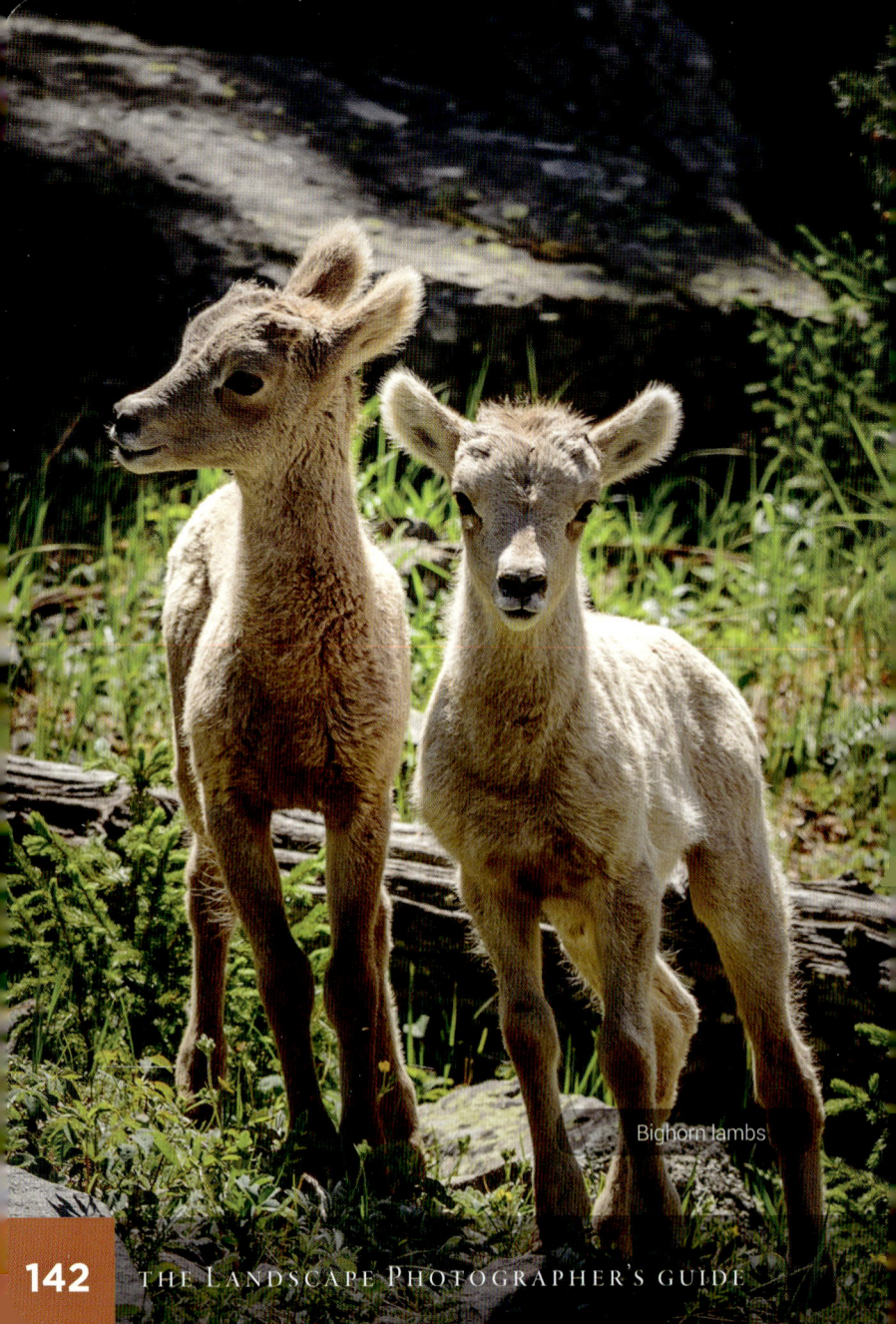

Bighorn lambs

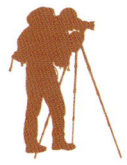

WILDLIFE

Rocky Mountain National Park is known for its abundant wildlife. Deer, elk, bighorn sheep, moose, coyote, and many other animals roam the park freely. This is a special place that has been set aside to preserve the natural state of both the wildlife and their habitat.

While Rocky is a great place to take wildlife photos, it must be done in a respectful way that does not habituate animals to humans or disturb them. This is not a zoo. The animals are not here for human enjoyment or for us to get photos of them. They are here because this is their home; we are the visitors.

In order to maintain this balance, the National Park Service has set some clear guidelines for how we interact with the animals. The first of these is quite obvious

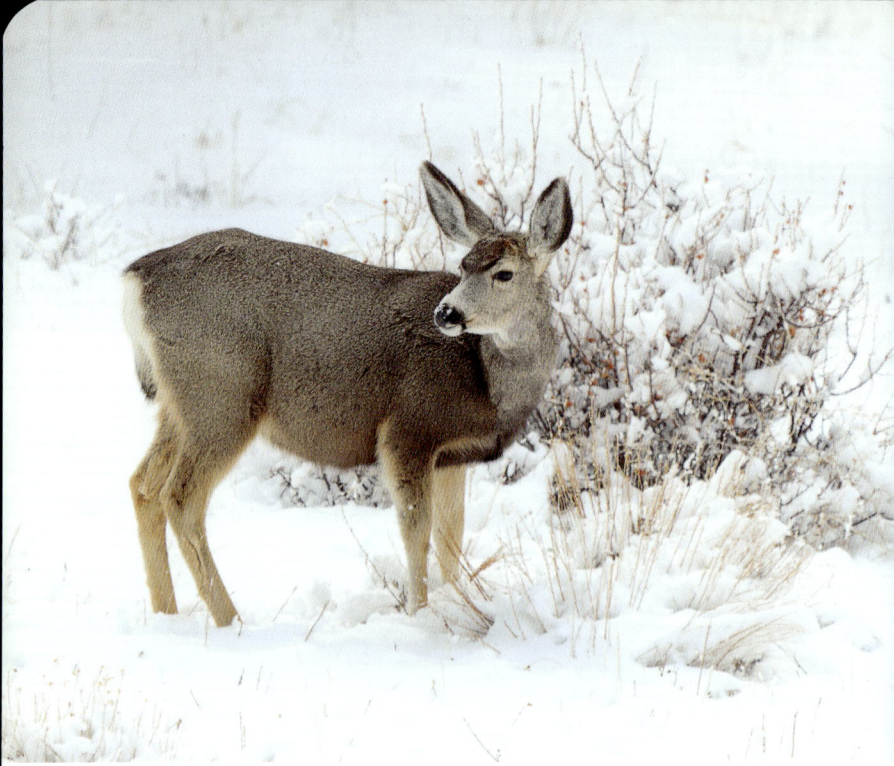

in that it is against park policy to feed the animals at any time. Feeding promotes dependence on humans. Moreover, the food we might give them could make wild animals ill. Some of the animals, particularly squirrels and chipmunks, carry numerous diseases and a simple bite could easily transmit them to humans.

The other and perhaps more difficult rule for photographers is that it is against park policy to approach wildlife. They are to be left undisturbed. If you find that animals notice your presence or begin to move away from you, then you have crossed the boundary of their comfort zone and need to move away. Each year people ignore this policy and some find themselves with very serious injuries. The best advice I can give you if you plan on photographing wildlife is to bring a very long lens. This will allow you to photograph your subjects without disturbing them or putting yourself in any danger.

Much like landscape photography, to get the best wildlife images you need the right light. Early morning or evening light with its warm, gentle hues will help make the very best wildlife images. This is also when a majority of animals are most active. At the same time, you need to pay close attention to the background. Since most animals are brown or gray, they tend to blend in with the rocks and mountains, so look for opportunities to photograph them with a contrasting background such as blue sky, white snow, green grass, or something else that will help them to stand out.

BIGHORN SHEEP

The bighorn sheep of Rocky Mountain National Park are one of the more elusive animals in the park and there is no guarantee that you will get a chance to see them.

During the late spring and early summer, they can often be found in the Horseshoe Park area at Sheep Lakes. They tend to come down to this little lake once or twice a day during this time of year to take advantage of the special minerals found here. The park service says that they typically come down between 9 a.m. and 3 p.m., so you will need patience and a bit of luck to see them.

Later in the summer, you can sometimes find bighorn sheep grazing in the tundra along Trail Ridge Road. A large herd of bighorn sheep live on Specimen Mountain, but because of their extreme discomfort with human activity, the entire mountain is off-limits to give them space of their own. However, they occasionally descend to the Colorado River on the backside of the mountain, so you may get a chance to see them if you hike the Colorado River Trail to Lulu City.

In the autumn, early winter, and early spring, bighorn sheep can often be found along Fall River Road between Nicky's Steakhouse and the Fall River Entrance to Rocky Mountain National Park.

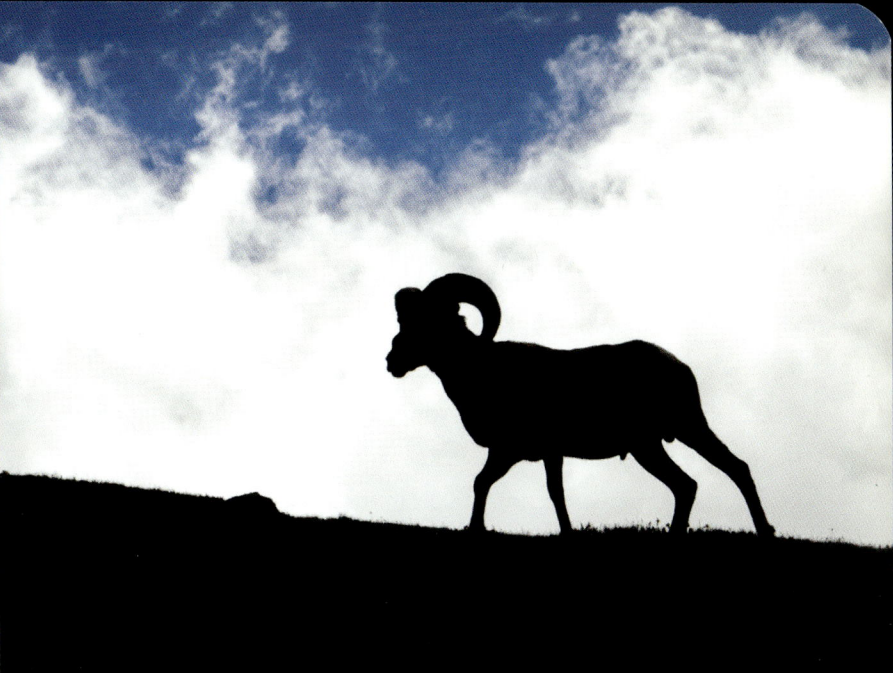

In the winter, a group of bighorns is also regularly seen licking salt off the road on Highway 34 between Estes Park and Drake, Colorado. If you decide to photograph here, make sure you find a safe place to park and pay attention to the traffic.

One of the challenges of shooting bighorn is that their coats are often dark brown or almost gray and they tend to blend in with brown grass and rocks. Ideally, you want to photograph them when they have snow, green grass, or blue sky as a background.

ELK

Probably the most popular animal in Rocky Mountain National Park is the elk. This majestic creature freely roams through the meadows, forests, and tundra of the park and is seen by almost every visitor.

In the winter, spring, and autumn, the elk are usually found in the lower meadows of Rocky Mountain National Park, often spilling into Estes Park and the surrounding area. As the temperatures climb in the summer, so do the elk. They make their way up to the cool tundra and can often be spotted alongside Trail Ridge Road.

In early spring, the elk can look quite shabby as they begin to lose their winter coats. At this time of year male elk often have no antlers, so this is generally not their most photogenic season. By late May, the elk are sporting their shiny new coats, and antlers are quickly growing while covered in soft velvet. Spring is also the time when elk give birth to their young. As a result, they can be very aggressive and will need to be given even more space than usual.

By July, the elk are often up in the high country. Along Trail Ridge Road you can sometimes photograph them using a long lens with Longs Peak or other prominent peaks in the background.

From mid-September until late October, the elk are

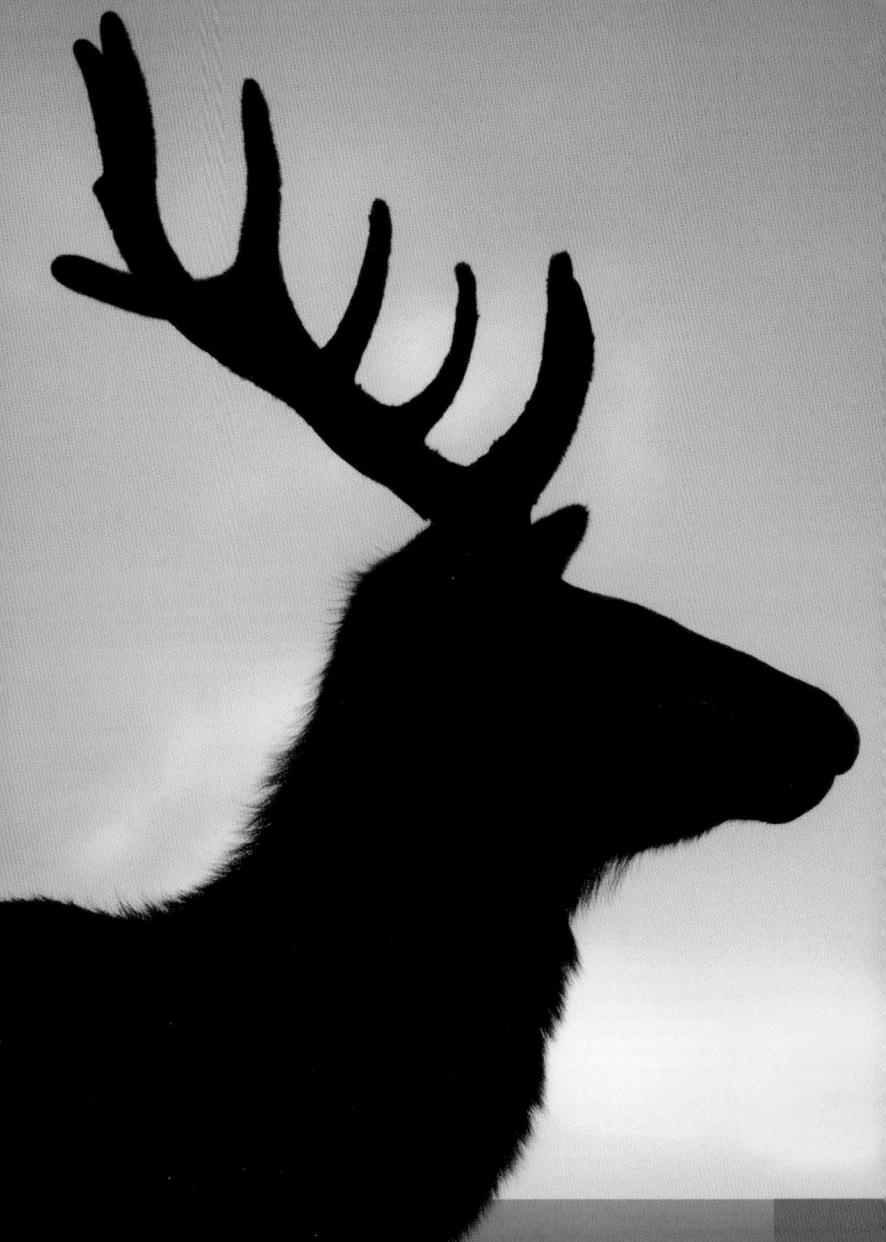

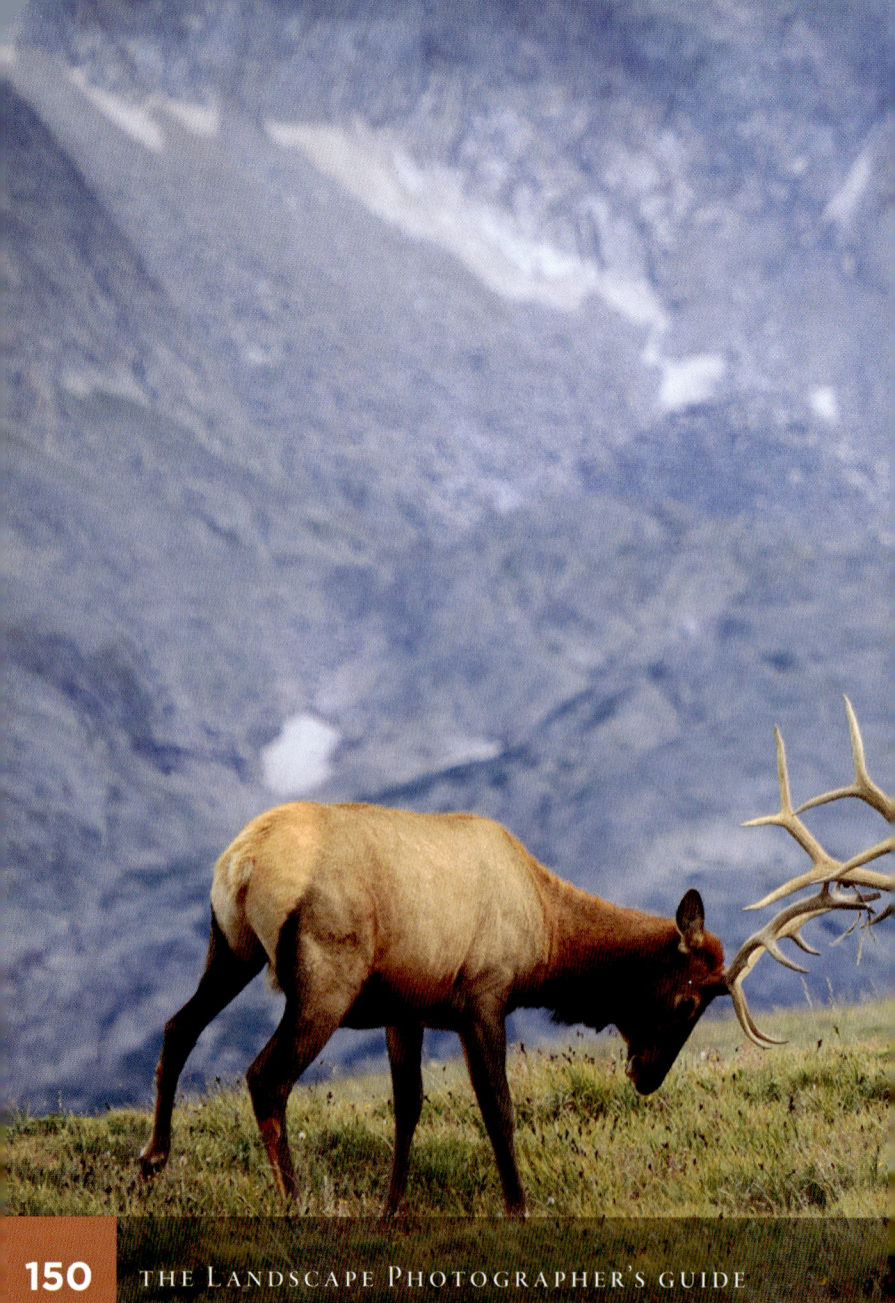

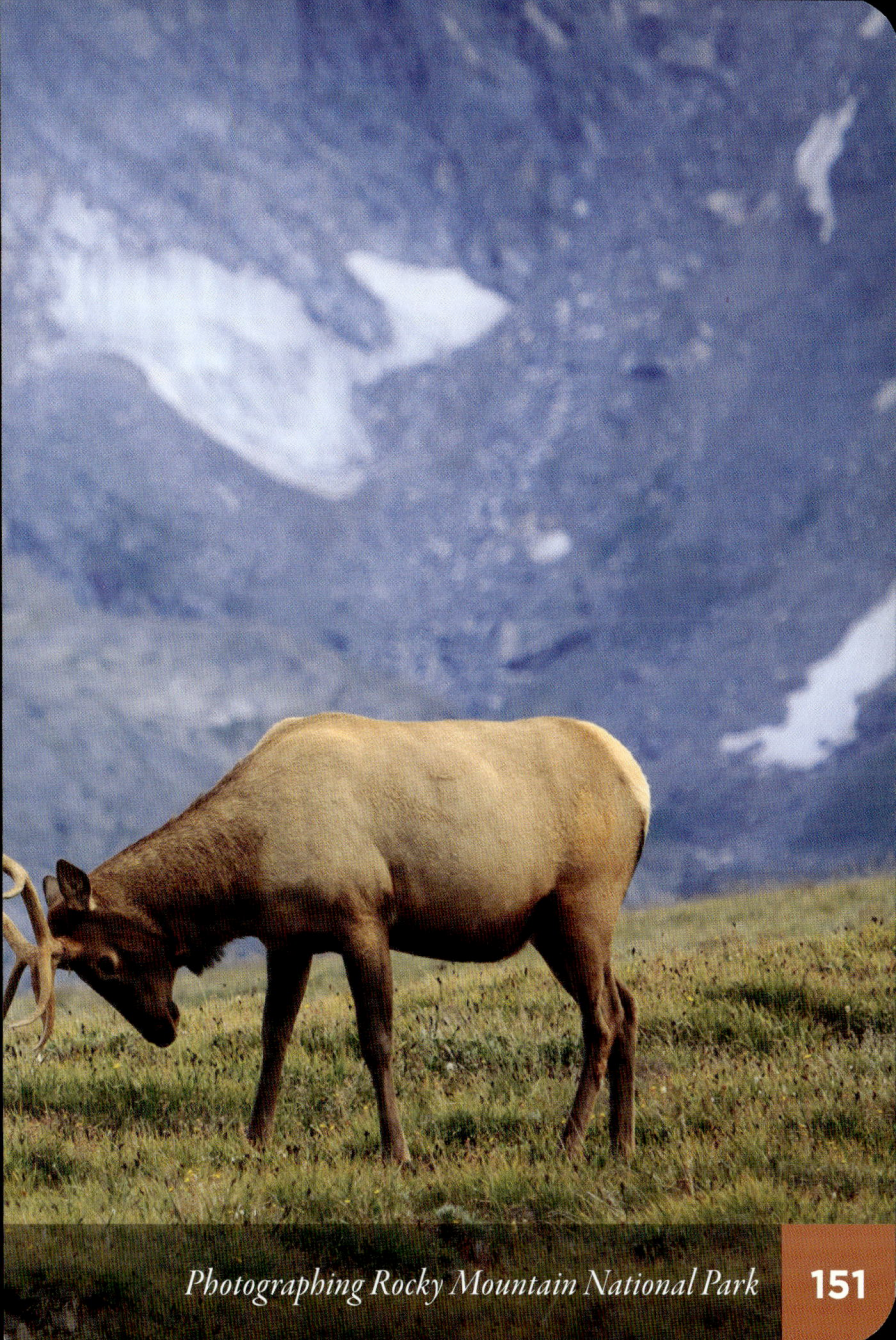

in rut. The male elk gathers his harem of females and spars with other males for control. This is a dynamic time and the air is filled with the sound of bugling. The best views are often found in Moraine Park, Beaver Meadows, Horseshoe Park, and the Estes Park Golf Course.

In the winter, they return to a more docile state as they forage for grass below the snow in the low meadows.

MOOSE

In 1978, the first herd of moose was transported from northern Utah to an area just outside of Rocky Mountain National Park. Over the years, these huge animals have multiplied and made their way into the Kawuneeche Valley on the west side of Rocky Mountain National Park. They like to inhabit marshy areas such as those found around the Colorado River basin. As a result, the best area to easily find them is right alongside Trail Ridge Road as it heads through the Kawuneeche Valley. They don't often stay right next to the road, so you will probably want to park at one of the many parking areas along the road and look out into the marshland for them. In order to get a good photograph, you are going to need a long lens, probably in the range of 300–600mm. Do not approach these animals; it is both illegal and very dangerous.

You can also find moose along the first couple of miles of the North Inlet Trail, the East Inlet Trail, and the Colorado River Trail. They can also sometimes be found up in Big Meadow, which is accessed via the Green Mountain Trail or the Onahu Trail. All of these areas are located on the west side of Rocky Mountain National Park.

Lately, more and more moose have been making their

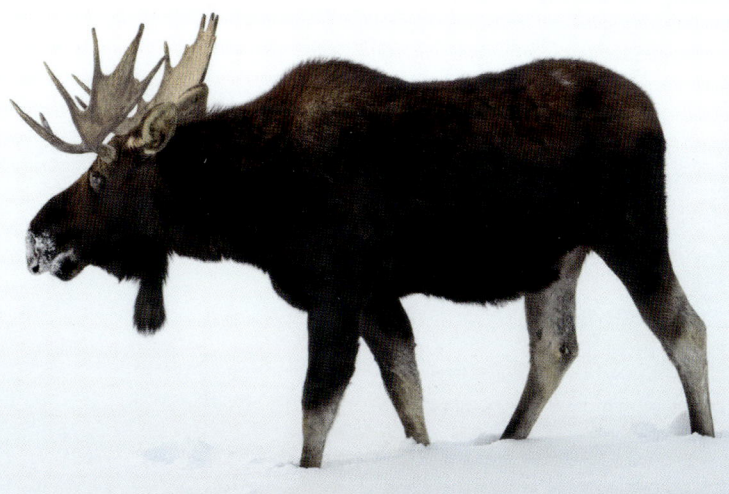

way across the Continental Divide and it is becoming more common to find them on the east side of Rocky Mountain National Park as well. They've been seen at places like Cub Lake, Sprague Lake, Bierstadt Lake, along Highway 7, and in Wild Basin. You might find them in almost any marshy area.

MARMOTS

Marmots are wonderful furry creatures that are related to squirrels, though they are many times larger. They generally live at higher elevations, usually above tree line. In the winter they hibernate and in the summer they tend to spend much of their day sunning themselves on warm rocks.

Marmots can be found all along the tundra sections of Trail Ridge Road. They seem to prefer rock piles where they can quickly find shelter, so anywhere you see a large rock pile above tree line you may find a group of marmots.

Marmots are regularly seen at Forest Canyon Overlook on Trail Ridge Road. Walk to the end of the path and there you might see them on the rocks at the end. Alternatively, drive to Rock Cut and you can often find them just below the wall on the south side of the road. They also seem to regularly hang out just behind the Alpine Visitor Center.

If you take the section of the Ute Trail that begins

across the road from the Alpine Visitor Center and follow the trail for about half a mile, you can often find a large number of marmots here. Please remember not to disturb them or approach them. They may seem cute and cuddly but they do bite and carry diseases. Give them space and photograph them in their natural environment.

Another way to find them is simply to listen for their high-pitched whistle while you are hiking. This is their warning system, much like that of squirrels. If you pay attention, you may even see pikas, relatives of rabbits that look like large round mice and are often found in the same rocky areas.

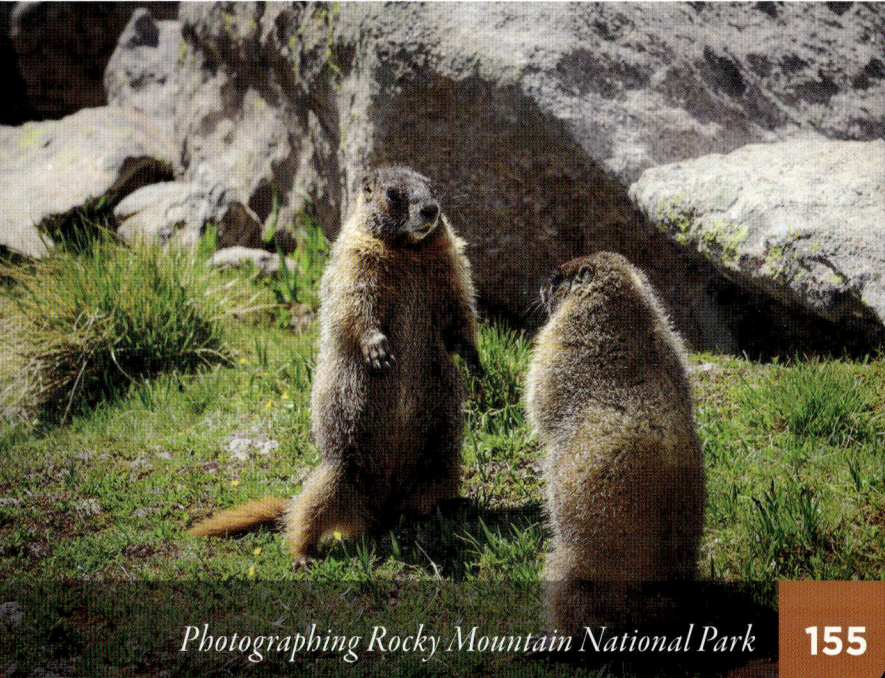

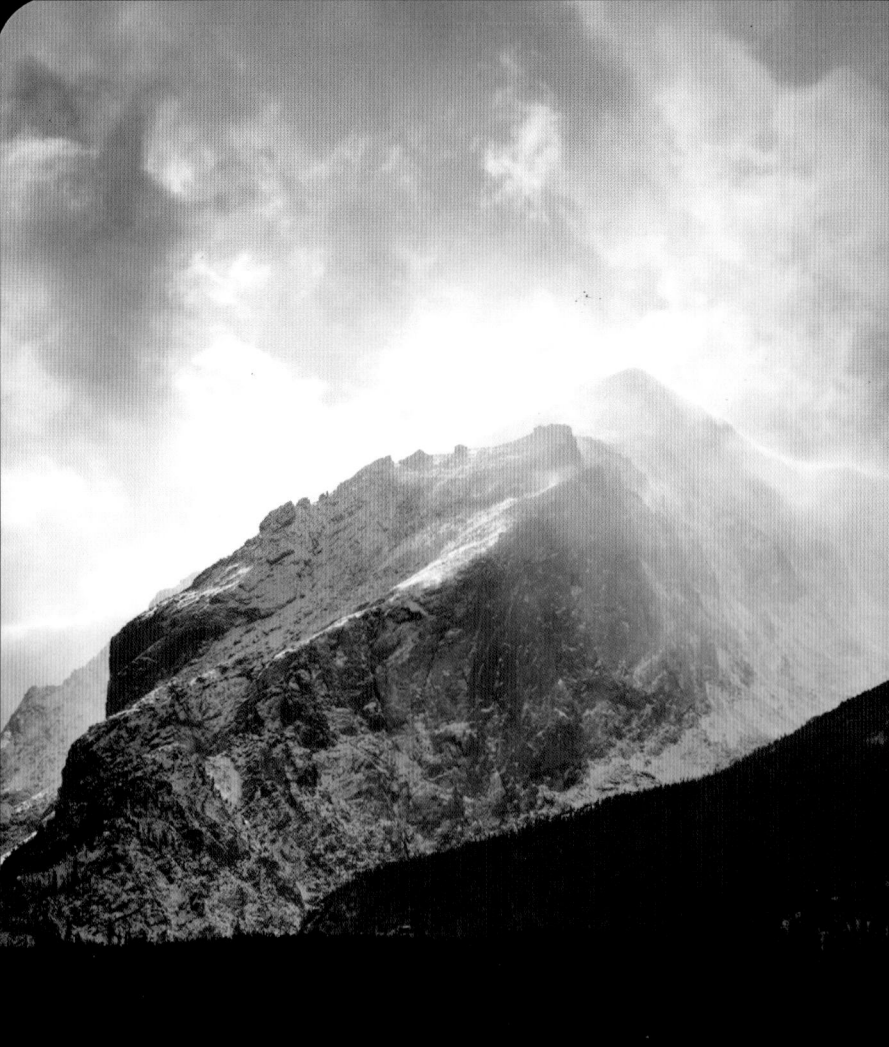

Hallett Peak from Beaver Point

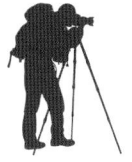

RESOURCES

This section provides some additional information and tools to help make your photography trip to Rocky Mountain National Park a success.

TOP LOCATIONS

If your time is limited, you probably just want to know where the very best places are to photograph sunrise or sunset. Below I have listed what I think are the most photogenic locations that I've ranked according to my own personal preference. Next to the location I've also listed the difficulty level of the hike so that you can make your own decision about which one would be best for you.

BEST SUNRISE LOCATIONS

These are some of the very best places to photograph sunrise in Rocky Mountain National Park. I've also listed the difficulty of getting to these places in time for sunrise. This doesn't take into account the difficulty of getting out of bed in time!

- Bierstadt Lake (Moderate) 38p
- Chasm Lake (Difficult) 79p
- Dream Lake (Moderate) 58p
- Gore Range Overlook (Easy) 105p
- Kawuneeche Valley (Easy) 112p
- Lake Helene (Difficult) 69p
- Moraine Park (Easy) 25p
- Sprague Lake (Easy) 33p
- The Loch (Difficult) 49p

BEST SUNSET LOCATIONS

These are some of the very best places to photograph sunset in Rocky Mountain National Park. If you plan to hike out to a location for sunset, remember to bring a head lamp!

- Bear Lake to Dream Lake (Moderate) 52-58pp
- Gore Range Overlook (Easy) 105p
- Grand Lake (Easy) 121p

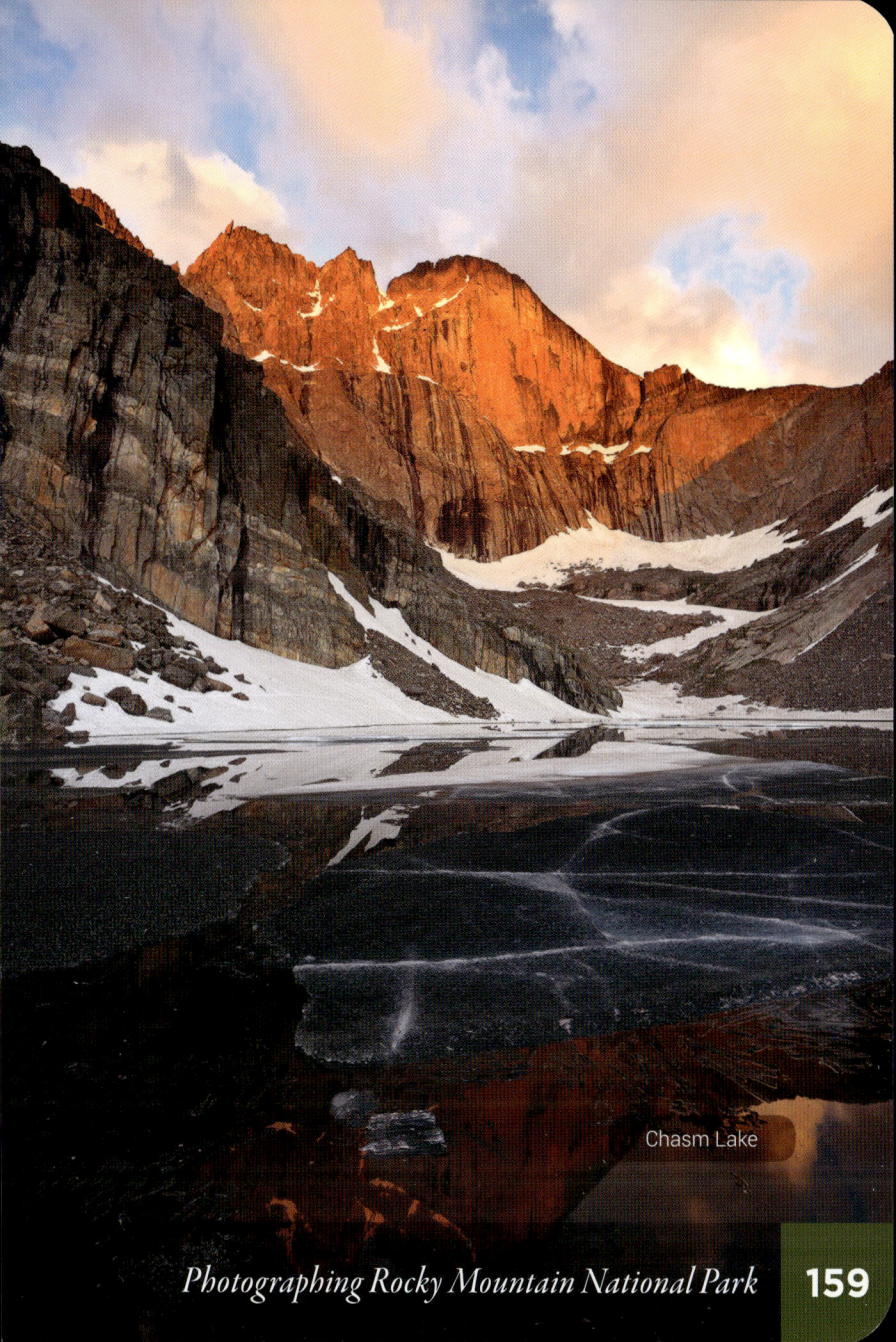

Chasm Lake

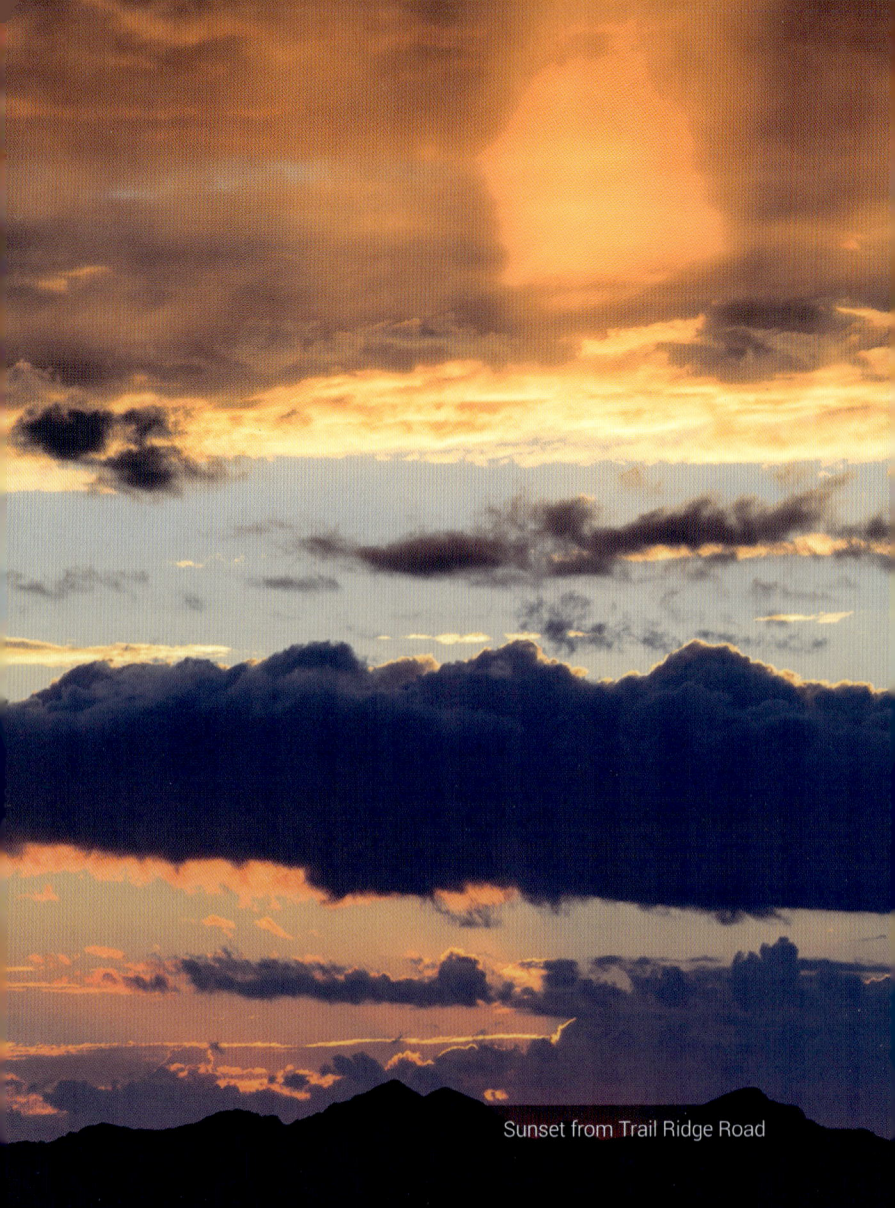

Sunset from Trail Ridge Road

THE LANDSCAPE PHOTOGRAPHER'S GUIDE

- Rock Cut (Easy) 102p
- Ute Crossing (Easy to Moderate) 100p

RECOMMENDED MATERIALS

- App: *The Photographer's Ephemeris* is an amazing app that I use almost daily to plan my photography outings. It overlays the direction of the sun and moon over a topographical map, enabling you to see where the light will hit during a particular time and day. It helps me to determine which locations will have the best light or when I can expect the light to be good for certain locations. It also includes an optional paid feature called Skyfire, which gives predictions for good sunrise and sunset light. The app is available for both iOS and Android devices.

- App: *Snapp Guides: Rocky Mountain National Park* — You can get all the information in this book in an app format. This allows you to click on any location to see it on a map and have your phone give you directions. It also includes additional photos to give you some other ideas and inspiration. You might even find some additional guides for other places that you visit. This app is available for iOS and Android through http://Snappguides.co.

- Book: *Rocky Mountain National Park: The Complete Hiking Guide* by Lisa Foster. This book is truly the ultimate guide to Rocky, covering nearly all of its 415 square miles. Even though it is geared toward the hiker, you will find lots of helpful information in here. I particularly appreciate the charts in the back, which contain the most accurate measurement of trails and elevations for planning your hikes.

- E-book: *Getting Started in Landscape Photography* by Erik Stensland. In this e-book, I walk you through how to take beautiful images of our natural world. I've kept the technical jargon to a minimum and focus primarily on how to use light and composition to create meaningful photographs while also covering topics like equipment and processing your photos.

- Map: Mountain Jay Media has produced an excellent set of topographical maps on Rocky Mountain National Park. They have one for the east side of the park and one for the west side. These are the best hiking maps I've found so far. They provide a lot more detail than the official park map that you receive when you enter the park. You can purchase these at any of the national park bookstores.

- Website: ClearDarkSky.com — This is one of my most used websites for planning photography outings. It provides a prediction of cloud cover. It is designed for astronomers, but it's just as helpful for photographers. It lays out all the information in a graph. You can then click on a particular hour to see predicted satellite imagery for that hour. I am generally looking for clouds over the mountains but none on the horizon where the sun will be rising or setting. I use this website in conjunction with many of the standard weather forecasting sites.

- Website: NPS.gov — This is the official website for Rocky Mountain National Park. Here you can find out current road conditions as well as updates on any area closures. The website has lots of helpful information about Rocky. One of the features I rely on daily is the system of park webcams. Currently, they have four positioned in various parts of the national park. These help me to see if there are clouds over the peaks, if there is a break in the horizon for sunrise or sunset, and also help me assess other weather conditions.

- Website: https://www.estesparkwebcams.com — This is a great website to see numerous webcams locations all around the national park. These can sometimes give a wider view of the area than you can get from cameras inside the park.

- Website: www.avalanche.state.co.us — The Colorado Avalanche Information Center is a website that many of us here rely upon in the winter to get the latest avalanche risk assessment. I don't head out into the mountains without first checking conditions here.

- Website: http://www.visitestespark.com — This is a great place to start when planning a trip to Estes Park. Here you will find accommodation and restaurant information as well as calendar information about what's happening during your visit.

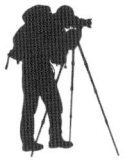

ERIK STENSLAND

Erik Stensland was born in 1968 in Minneapolis, Minnesota. He and his family soon moved to Montana, where he developed a deep love for the mountains. From a very early age he was hiking and exploring the streams and forests around his mountain home. In 1978, Erik's family returned to Minnesota, where he completed his early education. In 1991, after finishing college, he moved to Europe, where he met his wife, Joanna. They married and moved to the Balkans, living in Bulgaria, Albania, and Kosovo, where they spent twelve years assisting local churches and development agencies. In January 2004, they returned to the States for personal restoration and so that Erik could complete his MA in Organizational Development. They settled near Rocky

Mountain National Park in Colorado. Shortly after moving to Colorado, Erik decided to become a full-time landscape photographer. Having no professional experience in photography, he read books, studied the work of others, and sought input from professional photographers. Through this process of self-study and critique, he learned the basics of photography and began to build a substantial collection of work from Rocky Mountain National Park. In the spring of 2005, Erik entered the art-show circuit, selling his photography in shows throughout Colorado. His work began to be recognized and was soon carried by several galleries as well as purchased by companies ranging from McDonald's to Four Seasons Hotels. In April of 2007, Erik opened a gallery of his own work in Estes Park, Colorado. This gallery is the main hub for his activities. He has since opened a gallery in New Mexico and is planning others. Erik has also been building photography collections from the Desert Southwest, the Pacific Northwest, and the United Kingdom. Beyond photography, he is passionate about his faith and his family. You can see more of Erik's photography at his two websites: ImagesofRMNP.com and MorningLight.us. Erik also posts almost daily on his Facebook page: www.Facebook.com/MorningLightPhotography

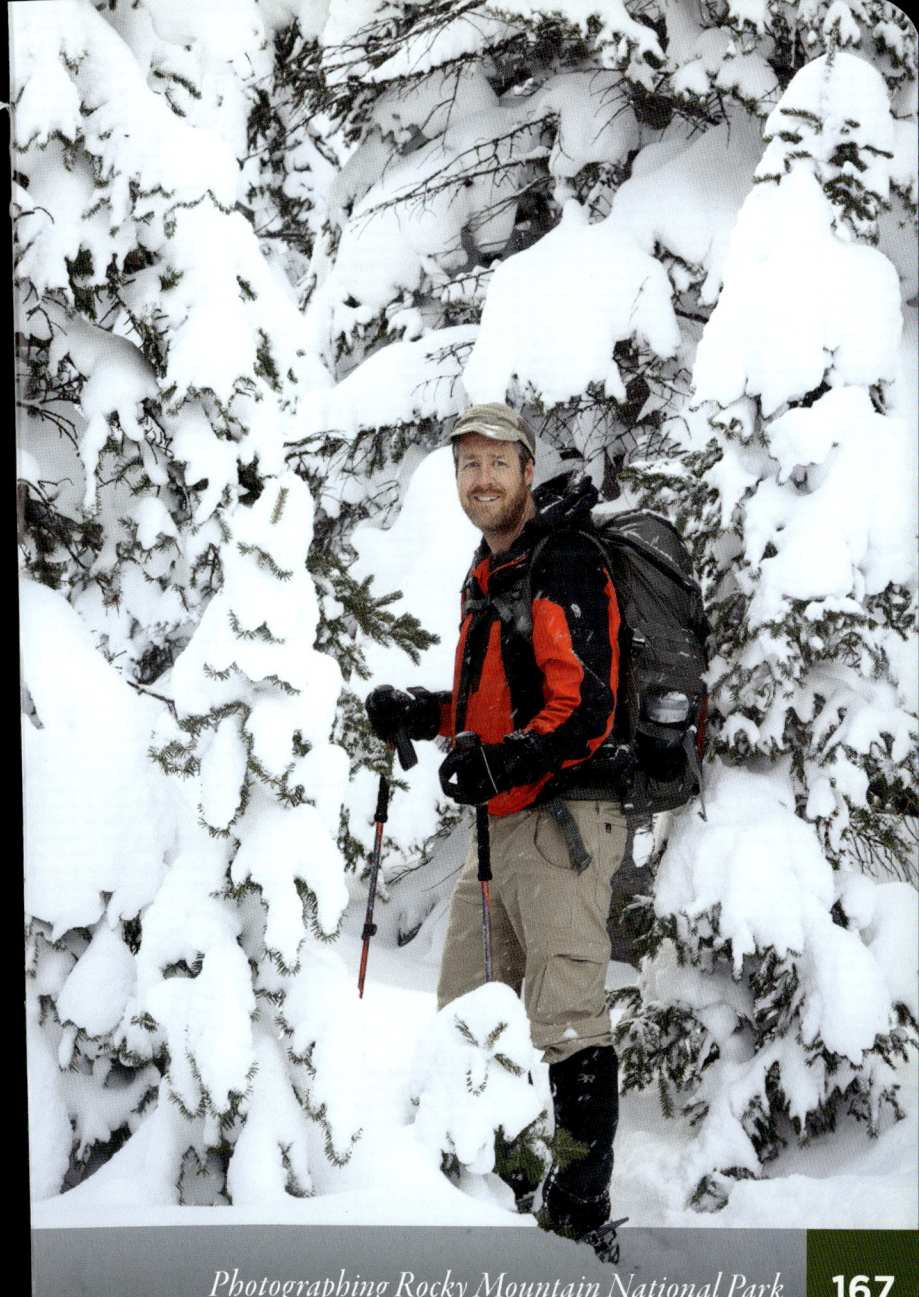

VISIT THE GALLERY

While you are in Estes Park, stop by the Images of RMNP gallery. Here you will find a large number of fine art photographs on display, as well as books, calendars, cards, and much more. It is a great place to find inspiration for your own photographic adventures in Rocky Mountain National Park.

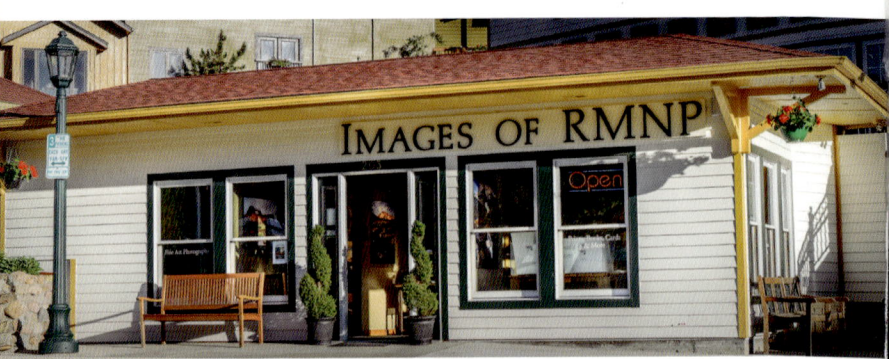

The gallery is located at 203 Park Lane, just behind Bond Park in the center of Estes Park.

You can also find Erik's images online at: www.ImagesofRMNP.com and on major social networking websites.